THE DIARY OF A GERIATRIC GOLFER

(Driving towards a sunset)

By Harry Pearce

**You know you are a geriatric golfer
when your walking stick
doubles as a five iron**

DRIVING TOWARDS A SUNSET

THE DIARY OF A GERIATRIC GOLFER

Preface and dedication

There are gangs of geriatric golfers (better known as 'seniors') all over the world. They all have their story to tell and secrets to unmask. This diary chronicles the adventures, misadventures, magic moments and monumental cock ups of one of these 'gangs' as they face up to the challenges of the game, the golf course and their age, (but not necessarily in that order!)

Above all, this diary is a celebration of playing golf as you head towards the twilight years of your life.

So thank you Pete, Kelvin, Hammy, Ray, John 1, John 2, Glen, Denis and Barry for your friendship and inspiration

INTRODUCTION AND HEALTH WARNING!

The stories you are about to hear are true.

Only the names have been changed to protect the innocent *

Like the legends of old handed down from generation to generation, they tell of a group of WOOPIES (Well Off Older People), who make a sacred journey every Wednesday to a tract of land in the middle of nowhere to practice the black arts of trying to hit a small white ball over three miles and into eighteen tiny holes in the ground.

This may seem pointless to the non golfer, but to these dedicated veterans it becomes a pilgrimage taking on an almost religious significance. Like the search for the holy - grail the 'G' golfer will explore every possibility, face intolerable frustration and leave no stone unturned to lower their scores, shoot par and beat the opposition into a pulp.

(* and if you remember the phrase *'only the names have been changed to protect the innocent'* from the 60's American TV series *'Dragnet'*, you would certainly be able to join us and qualify for the distinction of becoming a geriatric golfer)

Health Warning

Although the fellowship between this aging band of brothers is strong, from time to time the stress of trying to put the little white ball into the holes in the ground with less hits than anyone else turns them into rabid competitors, throbbing with jealousy, rage and self recrimination.

As yet there have been no major incidents of self mutilation or violence. (Although we have come close on several occasions)

But anyone on medication may have to read these chronicles with care.

THE VIRGIN GOLFER

I don't know how you were introduced to this wonderful game of golf, but for me it was the moaning and carping of an old friend, who will now become known as the *'Godfather'*, whose constant encouragement to turn up, flash the cash and give it a go finally paid off.

The Godfather is a slightly built, former rugby player, who had seen better days as one of the 'girls in the back row.' (This is a phrase that rugby players use to describe the more feminine members of the team who make up the backs, and recognizes that the real men in any rugby team are the brutes who make up the front row forwards). Anyway, the Godfather tells anybody willing to listen that he was pretty good at rugby once, and we try to believe him. This is especially true when it comes to the stories he remembers about what his team got up to in the bar after the games. You could even work on the assumption that earlier in his life, the Godfather was a 'first class piss artist' (in the nicest sense of the word). The fact that he had a major health scare several years ago and has still attempted to remain active is testament to his personality, good nature and ability to laugh at him self, a trait I soon discovered is vitally important when playing golf.

'Now you're retired … Come on …. Get with the old codgers, get with the *inn* crowd' he said referring to the age of everyone else and the fact that the nineteenth hole was often one of the main attractions for starting golf in the first place.

After two years of what can only be described as nagging, and the Godfather making me offers I could not refuse, I agreed to try the game of golf. The plans were made. Of course, anyone of advanced age mad enough to consider taking up golf has to think about the odds on certainty that they might make a fool of themselves, so I covered my tracks by saying I had never picked up a club in my life and that if I didn't take to it, I'd bow out gracefully. Secretly, being an ex PE teacher who thought he had an eye for a ball, I expected to pick things up quickly and give these well practiced amateurs a run for their money.

How wrong I was.

The day of the inauguration came and there I stood. No equipment. No idea. Not a clue: A bit like a lamb to the slaughter. My wife was very encouraging. 'Go on. Do you good' she said. *'**Get you out of the house.**'* Of course, the last reason (written here in bold italics) had more feeling and emotion put into it than practically anything else she had ever said to me. She even packed up a drink and a snack and patted me on the head like a little boy about to go on a school outing. 'Enjoy your self' she said closing the door quickly with an obvious sigh of satisfaction. She knew that if this golf idea worked out it would result in five peaceful hours every Wednesday.

I was picked up by another member of the golfing fraternity, now to be known as *'The Professor'* who was going to lend me his old clubs. 'A full set of irons' he said 'A driver and some woods' I pretended to know what he was talking about as I sat in the front seat of his BMW. ... 'Oh and a ball retriever' he continued with a glint in his eye.

The professor was another fully paid up member of the thinning grey hair and must wear glasses brigade, small in stature but powerfully built. He was a thoughtful friend and an ex cricketer and you could imagine him being good at golf. As I was to learn later ... What you imagine might happen and what actually does happen when you hit a golf ball, are often two different things.

To add to the newness of this fairly scary baptism into the murky territory of 'the swing', 'the rules', 'the etiquette' and the confusion of 'which club to use' came the fact that the professor was a fast driver and that the Lakeside Lodge golf course was hidden in the fens, down some winding, bumpy roads in a wonderful place called Pidley.

Pidley is a typical fen village with some interesting landmarks. The first you come across as you drive in from the east is a pub called The Mad Cat. It is a very famous pub that goes back generations. The name probably gives you some idea of the nature of the village. Pidley Horse Pond is the second major landmark and marks the turn you take to the golf course. It is where in days of old, the horses used to stop for water. Located between the pub and the pond is one of the most famous institutions in the village, an organization called *'The Pidley Mountain Rescue Team'*. Now, as you can imagine there aren't that many mountains in the flat land fens of East Anglia, so the concept of a mountain rescue team based in a landscape that only has a few dips in it is peculiar to say the least. Maybe the person who invented this strangely named outfit had a few too many down the Mad Cat Pub. But the rescue team does a magnificent job in raising money for charity and contributes massively to the social life of the village.

But back to my journey to my first attempt at the game of golf: The professor was driving faster. We turned right at the horse pond with a 'G' force equivalent to a rocket launch. As we bounced, swerved and squealed down a narrow track called Fen Lane, we could have been the lead car in a Raleigh competition. The clubs clattered in the back. I held on tight to the passenger safety rail. As we screeched to a halt in one of the parking bays, I felt sick.

The gang I have come to know and admire, (although I wouldn't admit it to them), were already there and to my untrained eye looked as though they knew what they were doing. Trolleys out, unfolded or assembled with consummate ease. Bags mounted on the trolleys with style, the clubs instantly accessible for these gifted amateurs. Golf shoes on and tied. Emergency moment: I didn't have any golf shoes but had brought some old football trainers. Would they let me play?

'You'll be alright for now' said a Scottish accent from a great character now to be known as *'Big Brother.'* Big Brother is six feet four with the eyesight of a hawk. If your ball is lost, call for Big Brother and the lighthouse will scan the horizon and pick out your ball with ease as if it's on some kind of homing devise. For this ability alone he is one of the most useful and most called upon members of the team.

So let me introduce you to the rest of the 'G' golfer gang:

First up: The short man in designer gear, with an artificial cigarette in his mouth. He was obviously trying to give up (and to this date has not succeeded). I noticed he had fewer clubs in his bag than anyone else and wondered why. He said 'hello' with a foreign accent and he will now be know as *'The Famous Belgian'* (mainly because we could never think if there were any other famous Belgians! Apart from Eddie Merks, Hercule Poirot and now the Manchester City centre back Vincent Kompany)

Standing next to a taxi, with a motorized trolley (that was forever conking out) a strongly built man who shall become known through this journal as *'The Monarch of the Glen.'* Like a well seasoned stag in heat (as in Sir Edwin Landseer's famous painting of a male deer proudly dominating a highland valley), he was always up for a rut or a bit of club throwing. He also had the interesting habit of smoking on the tee, sometimes quite literally after a wayward shot caused him to self combust. A natural comedian prone to farting, we always missed him when he wasn't there. He was always an important focus for a bit of chat, crack and flak.

Emerging from a new Jag with what looked like brand new set of clubs, another well built man. Let's call him *'The Rugby Man'*, a high achieving front row forward who knew the game of golf backwards. It occurred to me I didn't know the game of golf forwards or from any direction and here I was in the presence of obvious superstars.

In the distance, getting out of a four by four with a personalized number plate, a much younger character compared to the assembling group of grey skulls. He was a business man who worked hard and played hard and had the distinction of being awarded a black belt in Shotokan Karate. (So you can imagine how powerful he could be). From henceforth he will be known as the *'Karate Kid'*, not just because of his physical prowess but because, in the midst of the golfing turmoil we generated, he was a Zen - like figure, able to sooth the savage beast (mainly the Monarch of the Glen) with an aura of peace and tranquility.

I hired a trolley, with a feeling I must be off mine, paid for a round using a special half price coupon provided by the Godfather and made my way to the practice green. Everyone looked serious testing out what they called the 'speed of the green'.

'It's fast today.' Said big Brother watching his practice putt accelerate and disappear past the hole.

'Slow today.' said the professor noting that his putt held up a good six feet from the flag.

'Just right' said the Godfather as his practice putt made that wonderful plopping sound as it dropped into the hole. (Holding a putt, as it turned out, was a rarity for the Godfather)

Something in my imagination thought that the last minute of conversation had been lifted straight out of Goldilocks and the three bears, but instead of testing porridge, (too hot, too cold and just right), we were testing roll of a golf ball on a tiny piece of grass.

'What club do you think you will use the most' asked Karate Kid, making contact with me to ease my nervousness.

'Don't know' I said. 'It's my first time out' I must have sounded like a pathetic teenager on a first date or a prisoner on a day release.

'It's the putter' he said 'And what do we practice with least?'

'The putter?' I suggested.

'Correct' he said. It was the first of many valuable lessons I was given by the Karate Kid. Even though the putt seemed like the most natural and maybe the easiest shot in golf to get your head round, I have always remembered this first bit of advice and acted on it. I had a few putts, myself copying the bent knee 'poses' of the others who seemed to know what they were doing. Even without immediate success, at least the ball was going in the right general direction.

What followed the putting practice as we moved to the first tee can only be described as customized calisthenics for the elderly as we all engaged in what looked like a painful but minimal piece of stretching and swinging. Now, when you watch professional athletes warming up, you know that they look as though they know what they are doing and that the moves they make are deadly serious. They seem to bend the unbendable, stretch the unstretchable and reach the unreachable. The sight of a gaggle of geriatrics golfers wiggling, jiggling and niggling can only be described as ....*

(* Please insert you own words here as I lost the will to live when trying to think of one. Or if you can't think of an appropriate word, you could perhaps choose from the following options: Mind blowing; pathetic; ridiculous, drop dead gorgeous, minimal; painful; compellingly curious, laughable; comic; useless; absolutely riveting; about as useful as a chocolate teapot!)

Perhaps some of you have seen the Spanish golfer Jimanez warm up using a special pole as a stretching aid. (The fact that he does his warm up with a cigar in his mouth, however, suggests that he may not be taking the warm up as seriously as the sponsors of the pole would wish.) Nevertheless, we might suggest the idea of installing poles at various places along the course to the club captain. If the golf was proving a problem we could then divert our attention to pole dancing, something we are sure the Famous Belgian and The

Professor would be pretty good at. Some of the problems associated with this, of course, maybe where the pole would eventually end up and the fact that female foursomes may be pursued by male foursomes in the hope that the poles may inspire some erotic moves.

Back to the story: With the attempt at a warm up over, it was time to tee off. The Godfather took control. He is the traditional organizer and takes on the onerous responsibility of working out who will be playing with who. Why he has this role, I will never know, but his usual method is to sort out the groupings by putting random numbers next to random names. All eight of the geriatric golfers were there in force, so this would prove to be a big test.

'Give me four numbers between one and eight' he said.

The Professor called out 'One, five, three and eight'
There was a long delay.
'Give me the numbers again' said the Godfather in some confusion
'One, five, three and eight' repeated the professor.
There was another puzzled look as the Godfather tried to connect numbers to names and remember the sequence 'I can't work this out' he said much to the amusement of everyone else. It was then I realized that as we were all of a certain age, this was going to be one of many senior moments that would embrace us all.

The professor came to the rescue of his friend. 'I'll tell you what, Godfather. I'll play with the novice, you, and the Famous Belgian. The rest of you can tee off after us.'

The groupings had been set. The time had come: That moment when all golfers face their demons, no matter how experienced or skilful had arrived. We were on the first tee and looking good.

The Godfather was first. There was a tremble as he placed the ball on the tee, (later discovered to be the symptoms of a nervous medical condition). He took a couple of practiced swings which to my uneducated eye looked a bit strange. He settled, swung and sent the ball into the woods to the right.

'Out of Bounds' said Big Brother with just a hint of a chuckle in his voice.

The professor was next on the tee and looked smooth and capable. He nestled into his driving posture like a hen about to lay an oversized egg, snatched at the ball with a movement totally unlike the practice swings he had used and sent the ball into the sparse woodland to the left. 'Look at that' he said. 'What did I do that for?' No one replied. It must have been a stupid question.

The Famous Belgian was next. As a student of the mechanics and psychology of sport, I watched with interest as a swing which seemed to defy the laws of logic was practiced and delivered. He was starting from an almost side on position, his feet pointing at the woods to the left. The swing was very wide and rotational and to my PE educated eye, looked more like a discuss throw. Surely that would not work?

The ball went straight down the fairway.

'Typical' came the comment from the watching crowd. 'He thinks he's a guided missile'.

Then it was my turn. The Novice took to the tee. Felt nervous. This was virgin on the ridiculous so I asked for advice.

The Godfather was quick to chip in. 'Keep your head down. Keep your head down. Keep your **** ing head down.'

I wondered what coaching manual this pearl of wisdom had come from. I tried a practice swing. It felt awkward as I kept my ****ing head down. (I was later told by a coach to keep my ****ing head up). I decided to go for it. The ball sailed down the middle of the fairway.

'You've hit it as far as me' said the professor

'And a darn sight straighter' said Big Brother.
I felt good. The first shot was easy. Piece of cake.

How wrong can you be?

Without counting the air shots, which my new friends said I could take as practice swings, my card said 120 and counting. I was pleased they were taking pity on me.

I was on my way on this wonderful frustrating journey called golf. I hope you want to come with me.

STONE THE CROWS

The sixteenth at Lakeside is a par three of around 160 yards and always a challenge because the green is raised to stand perhaps six feet above the fairway. The border to the right is guarded by a ring of thick conifers, so if you go to the right, you can't get through them and have to go backwards (a common feeling for geriatric golfers). The border to the left is dotted with trees at fairway level, which can often block your shots to the green. Most of the geriatric golfers, by accident or design, end up well short of the green and use the normal excuse 'we were laying up.' As if anybody would really believe them.

The sixteenth is the hole where choice of club from the gang is most varied, ranging from a six iron for Monarch of the Glen and Karate Kid to a driver for The Godfather and the whole range in between. I usually use a seven wood and have ended up on the green only three times in two years.

Big Brother often uses a three wood. He settled down at the tee and committed to his usual classy practice swing, addressed the ball and hit a good shot just below the rise to the left of the fairway. We all tracked its flight, saw where it landed and applauded. 'Nice on Big Brother.'

A scattergun of shots followed at all sorts of angles from the tee, none of them any good, and we all moved off after our balls with Big Brother making a bee line for his superior position. When he got there the ball had vanished from the fairway. We all saw him pacing up and down and scratching his head. Bearing in mind that Big Brother sees all things at all times, we turned round to hear his Gaelic cry which sounded a bit like Braveheart going into battle 'It was there' 'It's gone.' 'That's impossible.'

We all joined the search for the missing ball with a growing disbelief that something so obvious could vanish and as if The Dark Lord from Harry Potter would sweep by any minute and claim responsibility for its disappearance. It was then we saw them: The flock of crows nestling in the rough to the right of the fairway. They were looking menacing, like a collection of attack birds from the Hitchcock film of the same name. They scattered when Monarch of the Glen sent his electric trolley towards them, and there at the centre, a full forty yards from where it had landed, and a much more difficult shot was Big Brothers' ball.

The Carrion crows had somehow morphed into 'Carrying' Crows. One of them had picked the ball up and moved it in a covert operation to its new position.

'Bastards' said Big Brother.

'No, Crows.' Said Karate Kid

'What happens now?'

No one knew. Was this a natural occurrence so BB would have to get on with it? Would relief be allowed? (And Big Brother needed some relief). Would we have to get the culprit crow to move it back? But the crows had moved on to the adjacent fairway and we were eyeing them up with contempt. The scene was set: Humans to the left and feathered enemies to the right. It was like an excerpt from the climax of a spaghetti western. All we needed was the Morricone music and a bit of whistling. Suddenly the crows started 'cawing' as if they were mocking us. 'Caw ... Caw ...' they screeched as the wall of sound came towards us. 'Caw caw .... That will give these humans a problem they deserve for taking over our native lands to play this game of golf.'

The 'caw, caw' was irritating, but what about the 'law, law?' What would the book of rules that no golfer can be without say about animal interference? ' Big Brother took the law into his own hands, picked up the ball and, I hasten to add, with NO CONSULTATION moved it back to the original position, saying he would get advice from the professionals at the club house after the game.

Whether he did this or not, I do not know … so I am asking the reader for help. If there is anyone out there who could advise, or has faced a similar situation (For example balls moved by Cheaters in South Africa, Anaconda's in the Amazon, earthworms in Ely or the dreaded lesser spotted ball catcher from Pidley), please keep this information to your self. Because if Big Brother ever found out that what he did was against the rules he would be not only be mortified to the point of self flagellation, but more importantly loose two shots.

Of course, this predicament became the overwhelming topic of conversation for the rest of the day. The gang exchanged ideas as they made their way to the final hole and in doing so opened up new areas of course management and golfing skill that had never occurred to them before: Namely the ability to train the local animals, without the knowledge of competitors, to move golf balls from bad lies to good lies, from lakes to land, from fairways to greens and from greens to holes. The realization took hold. This could revolutionize the art of golf into a whole new ball game: Birds popping up in mid air to stop a wayward shot going out of bounds, (Maybe the RSPCA would have something to say about that), Flying fish sacrificing them selves to stop balls from being lost in a watery grave. In time, through evolution and careful inter-breeding programs, this could result in brand new species of animals and plants highly adapted to the golf course*

Maybe we could reach the stage where actually hitting the ball with a club would not be necessary. Put it on the tee, call the menagerie into action and with no need to swing or hit anything, watch effortlessly as that little white ball make its way round the course on its own.

Eighteen holes in none.

* Some possible examples of highly trained birds that could be brought into play on the golf course. (With apologies to the RSPB)

The Get Out of The Sand Martin: A bird that miraculously removes your ball from a bunker. Limited use as only works for golfers called Martin

The Shoveler: A bird that gets you out of bunkers even if you are not called Martin.

The Hook Rook: Corrects hooking and slicing tendencies in mid flight. Requires danger money and training from an early age.

When I grow up, I'm going to be
A Hook Rook

The Great Tit of A Shot Changer: No explanation needed as great tits of a shot are well known on golf courses all over the world.

The Little Rake: Very useful as they rake bunkers for you

The Big Rake: For bigger bunkers

The Ball Hunting Reed Bunting: Especially useful when ball is lost in or at the edge of lakes

The Little Awkward and The Big Awkward: Deployed when you have a bad lie.

The Red Breasted Organiser: Keeps the score for you. Will cheat if necessary. Open to bribery

The Take The Piss Warbler: Attacks other golfers when they laugh at your shots.

The Stand Bag Pelican: Takes your clubs round for you. Makes better club selections than you.

The Short Tailed Plonker: Sings to you at the end of a bad round to make you feel better.

The Buff Breasted Take A Leak: Identifies when and where it is safe to relieve your self

The One Eyed Fly Catcher: Comes to your aid if you panic while taking a leak or pee into the wind.

The Thermal Tern: Doubles as a hand warmer and mobile base layer. Especially useful if you stick it down your trousers on a cold winters day.

The Great Bustard: Can be trained to crow at the exact time an opponent is taking a shot.

The Great Crapper: Hides ball of an opponent. Works best when you train a flock of Crappers.

A Great Crapper
waiting to unload

A Green Pitcher: Helps enormously with your short game.

The Little Tern. Ensures that if you hit a tree you get a members bounce onto the fairway

The Big Tern. As above but deployed when your shot goes deep into the woods.

The Wicked Tern. For extremely bad shots where the ball will be lost. This bird makes the sound of a ball hitting wood and then drops a different ball on the fairway.

The Arctic Tern. As above but migrates, and is only available in winter.

A Bloody Great Shag: Sometimes seen on golf courses. May bring back memories.

The Helmeted Caddy: An intelligent bird that can give you advice. Knows your game inside out. That's why they wear a helmet.

The Ordinary Caddy: Very rare because they don't wear a helmet.

The 'In the hole' Screecher: Migrates from America. Completely useless. Needs neck wringing.

The Oooh Me Goulie Bird: This bird is trained to fly at great speed into the nether regions of an opponent. Very useful if you are losing a match and want your opponent to retire hurt. Evolutionary experts are now experimenting by breeding birds with different beak types for maximum impact and collateral damage to the goolie area. Gives a new meaning to the term 'feeding the birds nuts'

If you can think of any more birds or animals that you would like available to you on the golf course, please add them here:

**A shoot the messenger bird bringing
Bad news on your new handicap**

A 'G' golfer in training

It also goes without saying that there are many different sorts of 'tits' on the golf course, some of which deserve a mention here:

The Great Northern Tit, which comes to the aid of golfers born to the north of Watford gap.

The Siberian Tit, for golfers who display communist tendencies

The Somber Tit, whose job is to lift your spirits after a bad shot. The services of this bird are much called upon in 'G' golfing circles.

The Willow Tit, which has a big pair of lungs and can suck the flight of an opponents ball towards the nearest Willow tree rendering their next shot much more difficult.

The Crestfallen Tit. A pet you can keep at home to console you when you come back with another bad score. Its call is similar to a human sob. (Aaaaah …. Aaaah ….. Aaaaah). It also produces real tears and tares your score card up for you to keep relining its nest

Although it may seem I am going on a bit (a characteristic of geriatric golfers who have nothing better to do) another three helpful bird species worthy of note are:

The Merlin. This bird lives up to its magical name and through its connection to the black arts, helps you make that miracle escape shot.

The Divot. Follows you around the course with the sole purpose of replacing the divots you make. A very busy bird.

The Buttock Clencher. Has a soporific song that lulls you into a false sense of security. Best deployed at the first tee to help calm your nerves.

MURDER ON THE FOURTH … BUT WE DIDN'T HAVE A CLUEDO!

I suppose in the history of golf, something like this had to happen to somebody somewhere on this planet, but that it should happen to us on a freezing day in February, year of our Lord 2013 was still momentous. Read on and see what you think.

We had ventured out into the icy blasts of the fens every bit as adventurous (or as stupid?) as polar explorers. We were well wrapped against the cold with plenty of layers, thermal long johns, chemical heat pads, woolly hats and ear defenders that made us look like roly-poly men in sumo wrestling suits. It was hard enough to walk and communicate, yet alone play golf. But at least it gave us an excuse.

The sun was breaking through as we reached the fourth and we were becoming immune to the low temperatures. The fourth is notorious at Lakeside as being the most difficult hole on the course (stroke index one) and is a hole where few of our kind have ever made par. After the events of this day, the fourth has now become even more notorious as the 'horror hole.' It will live long in the memory of 'those who were there.'

As usual we found ourselves facing down a third approach shot to the green, which hides alongside a large lake. It is always best for weak hitters such as our-selves to lay up into the narrow entrance to the hole and hope for the best.

The professor's drive and second shot were wayward and had taken him to the edge of the lake on the left had side. He had left himself the unenviable task of 'going over the wet stuff', which for geriatric golfers usually takes on the same degree of difficulty as Jesus walking on water. In other words, we usually need a miracle.

The professor took out a five iron and nestled majestically into the shot much like a mother hen laying an egg. The swing swished, the club head thwacked and the ball took off. From a side view we followed the flight of the ball in admiration and then lost it in the sunshine. All we heard was the beautiful 'thud' of the ball which we assumed had landed on the short grass for a tap in.

On reaching the green, the professor's ball was nowhere to be seen. Maybe it had rolled through? Maybe it had nestled in the laurel bushes at the side? Maybe it had disappeared amongst one of the many mole hills that border the lake? After a thorough search, it could not be found.

'But I thought it was *dead on'* said the professor

Little did he know how true his words would become and how they would come back to haunt him. Maybe he was psychic. Maybe he has the detection skills of Hercule Poirot. After a drop, which made his eyes water more than normal, we all scored badly and moved on to the fifth.

It was there we saw it: a dead Coote at the edge of the lake, fresh blood oozing into the water and turning it crimson. Feet splayed up like a dead fly. Beak still open from its last gasp of air. And there by its beak, the professor's yellow ball, the incriminating evidence of a murder.

The professor tried to deny it but the evidence was clear. Obviously the 'thud' we heard was the ball hitting the body of this unfortunate bird, probably in flight, or perhaps the thump of its deadly landing.

So in fine CLUEDO tradition, we make the following declaration:

IT WAS THE PROFESSOR, WITH A FIVE IRON, BY THE LAKE.

**The professor tries
out his new club**

The story has already passed into geriatric golfer's folk lore, much like the stories of the heroes and villains of old. (Geriatric golfers will remember well the stories of Noggin the Nog!). There is no doubt in similar fashion it will be handed down from generation to generation. Plans are being made to erect a small memorial at the site of the dastardly deed and each week we play, it grows in size. There have also been rumors that Quentin Tarrantino wants to by the film rights under the working title of Reservoir Frogs.

Since this act of violence we have also noticed that as the professor approaches other wild life on the course they move away with unusual haste. His infamy and violence towards other creatures has obviously been spreading. And every time we pass the spot where the body was discovered we bow our heads and remember 'murder on the fourth.' The professor, the perpetrator of this foul deed also bows his head, not in memory of the dear departed bird but because the little Coote made him drop a shot. The professor is a hard man.

THINK NEGATIVE

Warning: If you are of a nervous disposition or easily offended, it may be advisable to skip this chapter as it contains allusions to and real cases of blasphemy and swearing.

It is encouraging to observe how the friendship of our Band of Geriatric Brothers has evolved. In the face of adversity we have bonded into a lean mean fighting machine, ready to support each other through all of the crap shots we regularly play. Although golf is an individual and competitive game, the geriatrics know they will always have the undying support of their friends as they cope with the frustration and despair that the game of golf can bring. To use a psychological term: When the going gets tough the tough get going. We give each other 'positive strokes', 'big ups' and 'warm fuzzies' in a constant effort to get us through a nightmare round.

There are many examples of this ongoing support. The positivity is endless, no matter how bad the shot. For example, comments that make you feel better when your careful swing take a large divot out of the fairway and send the ball five yards further on 'At least the direction was good' says the Famous Belgian to lift your spirits for the next attempt. If you are lucky, he might even replace the divot for you

Or when you zig - zag down the course from one side to the other, from rough to rough. The pain of turning a 360 yard hole into a 500 yard one is tempered with the softly delivered comment 'At least you are going in the right direction.' What a blessing it is to receive such comments as you trudge from side to side.

And there in the background is the Godfather, smoothing your incredulity as you top the ball and send it into the bunker forty yards in front. 'Looks like you might have a good lie' he says softening the blow and giving the illusion that everything will be alright.

'Good length' says the professor as your putt goes pin high but has all the direction of a wayward electron in the Hadron Collider and ends up seven feet from the hole.

'Good Line' says Big Brother as the putt is so powerful that it skirts around the hole and disappears into the rough on the other side of the green.

'Think positive' says the Karate Kid as you suffer from the 'yipps' and send the ball thirty five degrees off course into the woods. He continues with his altruisms: 'The greatest distance in golf is between the ears.' This is normally a useful piece of advice but you can't help thinking that all you've got between your ears at the moment is mush.

Or how about this situation we have all faced: It's an important hole. You have a tap in from two feet. You miss. You emit a bellow of despair from your inner soul and wait for the comments of disbelief. But instead of mockery you get wise explanations: 'The grass on this hole is always a problem' says the Godfather. 'About time they sorted it out.' 'G' golfers are masters at deflecting the responsibility of a duff shot onto grounds men.

G Golfers are by their very nature full of advice and after care. But there came the day when we decided to try something different.

'For once, let's forget all this positive stuff' said The Monarch of the Glen as another of his drives went more sideways than forwards 'It's doing my head in. For once, let's call a spade a spade. If its crap, tell it like it is. **THINK NEGATIVE.**'

We took up his suggestion with gusto as if all our creative abilities, that had been shackled for so long now had the chance to escape. There followed and amusing interlude of cutting remarks, humiliating comments and obscenities the like of which have never been heard on the golf course before and may never be heard again. A few of the more printable are posted below. They were often accompanied by laughter, cat calls and insults. Sometimes the mockery started before you took the shot. For once the etiquette of golf was forgotten and stone- age man took over.

'THINK NEGATIVE!' said the Monarch

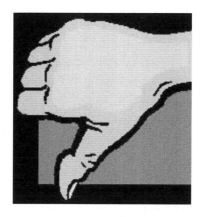

'That's the crappiest shot I've seen in my life'

'That chip has earned you the dick head of the day award'

'Call that an f****ing swing. My grandma could have done better and she's dead.'

'After a shot like that have you ever considered giving up?'

'What kind of stupid **** er plays a shot like that?'

'The way you are playing, aim for the bunker, you are bound to miss it.'

'That putt was basically bollocks'

'If I was you, I'd pray for a f***ing miracle.'

'Twenty years of dedication and you still play like a prat.'

Or this situation: Everybody is waiting. Because you have been playing so badly you decide to concentrate just that little bit more. You slow things down and take some extra time on the tee, do a few practice swings, go into that zen –like stillness you need to hit the ball properly. Despite all this preparation, mind control and 'posing', you send the ball wayward into the woods and out of bounds. 'Well, that was worth waiting for.' Says the Monarch telling it like it is.

But what a day it was. As a one off occurrence, this focus on insults and negativity produced one of the most interesting and humorous rounds of golf we have ever played. When the conditions are right, why not give it a try. We found that geriatric golfers, although wobbly on the skills of golf are experts at negative comments and negative thinking. Maybe you will want to follow our lead or have done this negative thinking thing already, but if you are new to negativity, make sure you agree it first!

To continue with the negative creativity theme, what follows are two songs dedicated to all negative thinking 'G' golfers everywhere. The first is roughly based on the Elvis Presley Song 'It's now or never' or 'Ol Sole Mio' or that famous ice cream advert with the same tune.

CHORUS.

It's now or never
You'll miss the ball
Your swing is rubbish
Your putts all stall
Tomorrow will be the same.
Give up you dick head
Give up the game.

MAIN VERSE:

You are a golf bum
And you always blast one
Into the long grass
Might as well shove it up your a***
Please take the five wood,
Swing it where the ball stood
And if it hits
You'll have the yipps,
Balls lost again

REPEAT CHORUS above.

The second is this song loosely based on 'These Foolish Things Remind me of you' by Fred Astaire:

Your two foot putt is stroked with no direction
Your chip towards the green is imperfection,
Your three wood hit, is shit.
These foolish things remind me of you.

You look so good when you are practice swinging
But when it is for real, your shot is 'minging'
If only you could play,
These foolish things remind me of you.

Although your scores are crap, you don't stop trying,
And you will not improve, so please stop crying
And you will just get worse,
These foolish things remind me of you.

A slice into the rough and you're past caring
And all that you've got left are grunts and swearing
We know you try your best,
These foolish things remind me of you.

This is the way it is with geriatrics
When all that you've got left is golf's 'theatrics'
And so you throw your clubs,
These foolish things remind me of you.

We all have medical needs with complications
And warm up body parts with slow gyrations,
We might as well be dead,
These foolish things remind me of you.

At last, the eighteenth hole and you're still standing
You'll make it to the bar with a tough landing
And then you miss 'your round',
These foolish things remind me of you!

When Will You Become a Geriatric Golfer, Or Are You One Already?

Like death and taxes, growing older will happen to us all as we reach the slippery slope of inevitable decline and start speeding down it towards the sunset. But how do you define that fearless bunch of players who keep going after all hope is lost so they can become blessed with the title of a 'Geriatric Golfer'? Here are some possible definitions. Maybe you could add your own:

A person in the twilight of their golfing career: This is a gentle definition for someone who has basically lost the plot, plays crap most of the time, and has added an average of ten shots to their game as they have got progressively worse.

Someone who has definitely seen better days: Another gentle definition for a terminal condition. Please note that as we start losing brain cells, skin tone and muscle elasticity from the age of nineteen, this condition could begin to emerge from the age of twenty. Some people over the age of sixty can't even remember if they ever had 'better days'.

A formerly confident and energetic human being, whose mental and physical capacity is shot and who have to spend at least thirty minutes trying to get out of bed in the morning .

A geriatric golfer can be someone who, when they finish eighteen holes, sits down at the bar for a drink and then struggles to get up. Please note: This attempt to rise from the sitting position after playing is often accompanied by the well known *'cry of the geriatric golfer'* as joints seize up and muscles tense. It goes something like this ….. ' OOOOOH; …… AAAAAAGH; ….. OHNOOOO; … JUST GIVE ME A FEW MINUTES.' They then have to sit back down and try not to dribble.

Once in the standing position, they then have to psyche themselves up to take the short walk back to the car and frequently can only do this by using their trolleys as an extra support. The main characteristic of the geriatric golfers walk after playing eighteen holes is that they are often forced to carry out this most basic of human skills without the ability to bend their knees. When you add to this straight legged shuffle the tell tale signs that their circulatory system is in closing down, they often look like a line of zombies from the film 'Dawn of The Dead' roaming around in straight lines with nowhere to go. In fact in these hard times, it is probable that the next Zombie film will recruit their extras from a cast of geriatric golfers. They are already well trained in all Zombie like movements and the film makers will have to spend less money on the make up.

A 'G' Golfer: Someone who after nine holes, struggles to reach the tenth.

In extreme conditions someone who after the first hole struggles to reach the second tee (especially if it is uphill)

A person who after a night of not sleeping well, cannot find the first tee.

A person who needs help to put their golf shoes on. These people are often seen wobbling by their car and using the back bumper as a leg hoist. Standing on one leg is very difficult for a 'G' golfer.

A person who evokes pity as they fail to bend down to remove the golf ball from the hole and after several attempts, has to get down on their hands and knees. This definition extends to golfers who have trouble with balance and put themselves in danger when retrieving a wayward ball from a ditch or a lake. This lack of hand – eye coordination also results in them missing the ball and scooping up mud or pushing the ball even further into a murky grave.

Someone who turns up on the wrong day or at the wrong time or on the wrong course and blames everyone else

The stupid bugger who forgets their clubs: (This did happen to the Godfather and marked him out as a geriatric golfer). He stood at the car, opened the boot and saw nothing. 'I left them in the garage' he said. 'Along with the brains' we said.

The Karate Kid, the youngest of us all, once showed fairly extreme geriatric tendencies when he turned up on the first tee in his slippers. As a business man he is often late and preoccupied with sorting things out. He had obviously left the house in his slippers without realizing, driven the four by four without realizing and grabbed his golf equipment without realizing. The hallmark of the G Golfer is that they don't realize very much at all even if it's staring them in the face. Of course, being a natural problem solver Karate

Kid went into the pro shop and bought a new pair of golf shoes immediately.

A 'G' golfer: Someone who can't see his ball on the fairway and walks past it.

A 'G' Golfer: Someone who not only can't see his ball on the fairway, but grinds it into the ground with the wheels of his trolley.

A person who tries to put his club in the wrong bag or ends up pushing the wrong trolley: (This usually goes uncorrected by the other geriatric golfers who use it as an opportunity to point, laugh and mock.)

This true story from the first tee will demonstrate beyond doubt the condition of a geriatric golfer: It involves the Godfather. He had, for a change, hit a masterly shot down the fairway. We all complimented him on its direction and carry and set off on our merry way wishing each other 'bon chance' 'have a good one' and other inane motivational comments.

It was Godfathers turn to take his second shot, but he stopped dead in his tracks. 'I've let the driver head cover on the tee' he declared as if it was the end of the world. Without further thought, he turned round and was trotting off back to the tee in search of the missing piece of fabric.

Now, the Godfather's drives at best are around 160 yards and this was a good drive, which meant there were 160 yards to the tee and 160 yards back. This is a long way in the life of a 'G' golfer. We all waited, relieved that no one was following us and therefore would not be able to accuse us of slow play, and the Godfather was trying to run. Now, the sight of a geriatric golfer running is a sight to behold. 'Normal' running means that people raise their knees, elongate their stride and eat up the ground in wonderful bouncing strides. For example: Usain Bolt, the 100 meters record holder from Jamaica knows how to run and you marvel at his grace. 'Geriatric' running is the opposite and the Godfather' style was more like 'shot his bolt'. Knees stay on the horizontal, strides are measured in inches and bouncing becomes a barely visible bob. An ordinary walk might have been quicker.

Still, he made it back to the tee. We could see him looking around and realized that this was only half the journey and he would have to make it back. It was Godfather on the run part two. But The Godfather was beginning to struggle and even at that distance we could see his rosy red cheeks blowing and his little legs faltering. Big Brother checked he had his mobile phone to hand, just in case we had to call the emergency services and we watched his slowing progress as he came closer and those mini strides got even shorter

After a few minutes he was back with us but barely in the land of the living. His lungs were on maximum as he gasped for air. His little cheeks were crimson. Pulse rate was throbbing. We later had the thought that it might be a good idea for one of us to be appointed as first aider with the ability to give mouth to mouth and cardiac massage, because the Godfather was struggling to reach his second shot, yet alone take it.

After a slow recovery he was able to speak between gasps.

'Head Cover ….. wasn't …. there' he said. 'After all that, …. the bastard thing …… wasn't there.'

Knowing the Godfather, we decided to check his bag. For some reason he had zipped the head cover away in one of the pockets for safe keeping.

'It was here all along' said Big Brother with benevolent understanding

'What am I like' said the Godfather.

'A geriatric golfer' we said.

The principal is now well established. Ritual humiliation is part of a geriatric golfer's lot and the quicker you get used to it the better.

**But I only left my head cover
On the first tee**

The godfather also has starring role in the continuing saga of the lost gloves or the more apt title: 'The phantom glove snatcher of

Lakeside Lodge': On numerous occasions (too numerous to mention here) the Godfather has suddenly panicked and told us all that he has dropped his glove on the last green and must return to find it. There is a look of such desperation on his face that we always take pity. This search for the missing glove has several routine endings:

He finds it in his back pocket (where he always puts it when he putts) and it is not, in fact, lost.

He has dropped it and with no awareness treads on it as he retraces his steps

He is still wearing it

He forgot to bring his gloves in the first place and it's taken him the front nine to realize

He has actually lost it.

With all these variations to a common problem, and the fact that the Godfather has this inbuilt ability to lose things or forget things, we now make sure that someone walks behind him as he 'wends' his way round the course.

'Wend' is a particularly good word to use to describe the movements of 'G' golfers in that it suggests we make our way around the golf course without much purpose and even if we do have some sort of purpose, that purpose rarely works out. So …
'wending' is what we do. It is the default method of travel.

'Wending' also has several attached activities:

The 'wildlife wend' which includes a focus on nature so you can observe the wildlife as you move between shots. Big Brother is particularly good as this form of 'wending', especially if his ball has ended up in one of the many lakes around the course. His ability to spot and identify fish is unsurpassed. I must also comment here that lakeside Lodge in Pidley is a superb place to wend round and a definite plus when playing golf.

The 'Comedy wend' which includes the telling of jokes (too blue to be recorded here). The Karate Kid is an expert at this form of 'wending';

'The change the world wend' when you discuss issues of vital concern such as …. Is Obama doing a good job? How you would sort out the Euro problem, your solutions for Afghanistan. And with all this talk to change the world, you never bear in mind that the most important decision a 'G' golfer might have to make that day, is what time they will go to bed.

The oblivious 'wend', where you move into the line of fire of an opponent without realizing it. We are all guilty of this lack of observational skills when on a 'wend' and it is only cured when someone has the presence of mind to shout 'heads up, plonker' (or words to that effect). This has the effect of turning the 'wend' into a run for cover.

Another form of wending often experienced by 'G' golfers is called the **'Knackered wend'** when you are so tired from your exertions that it seems you do not realize which direction you are going in or where your ball is. This is often accompanied by the loss of your ability to count and a tendency to forget duff shots. Other golfers will not allow this loss of memory to happen.

Of course not registering a duff shot, losing the score, recording a wrong score are cardinal sins that remain unforgivable by any golfer and particularly a 'G' golfer, and I must admit, as a novice I suffered from this inability to keep the score. The fact that I have a condition known as discalculus doesn't help. (The inability to do mental arithmetic, work with, see or retain numbers).

But we have all done it, haven't we? … Finally got the ball in the hole and then realize we don't know how many shots it took to achieve this miracle. In a painful retracing of steps, in our minds eye, we work our way back down the fairway reliving and trying to forget the moments of doom and then come up with a number that is wrong. I did this more than most when I was learning but with the guiding hands (if you do that again, I'll slap you), the biting lips (I saw what you did, you golfing heathen) and the potentially venomous tongues (are you sure you got a par, you *****) of my fellow 'G' golfers, I am getting better. (By the way the ***** in the last bracket was always unspoken but sometimes displayed in the body language and the eyes)

The psychological principle is clear. On your score card, it is easier to forget a duff shot than a good one. On someone else's score card it is easier to forget a good shot than a duff one. How Machiavellian this world of golf can be. But 'G' golfers rise above it.

....

But we must not only focus on The Godfather for stories of senior moments. Even the Professor has suffered from an embarrassing memory glitch and he is the last person you would think of as someone who would lose the plot.

Maybe you have had this feeling too: Somewhere on the journey around the golf course you have lost your set of house keys and car keys. You thought you put them in the special compartment of your golf bag reserved for important things, but they are no longer there. You check the compartment again and it is definite: they are not there. Your life flashes before you as you begin to realize the implication of being 'keyless'. Maybe they fell out of your bag onto the course, so with this in mind, you begin to retrace your steps in an impossible search. Your fellow 'G' golfers help you in your quest, turning over leaves, trying to remember where you took your shots from, looking forlornly down the fairway at any likely looking object. All to no avail.

In the end you accept your fate and resolve to finish the game and report it to the office when you leave, in the hope that some kind soul will have found them and returned to base.

But nothing is that simple and your keyless life remains on hold. There have been no sightings of your keys anywhere. (Maybe it was the crows again, getting their own back … see an earlier chapter). After the game a fellow geriatric golfer offers to drive you home so you can get the spare set of car keys (if you can remember the safe place you keep them) and in a depressed mood you trudge to the front door ready to tell the wife what a plonker you have been.

Later you find out you have been an even bigger plonker:

Your wife checks your bag with that condescending 'woman's touch'. She finds the keys. The keys were in the golf bag all along and, to cap it all, they were in the special compartment you always use. The one you checked so many times. 'How could this happen?' you cry. The answer is simple. It's just that you lost all senses in your fingers and were unable to detect them. This is a symptom of old age: You see things when they are not there and can't see them when they are.

After a quick cup of tea and lovingly made sandwich, your wife takes you back to the golf course in her car with that smug look on her face that says 'Why on earth did I marry you?' 'If I'd have known you would have turned out like this, I would have married my other boyfriend.'

'What other boyfriend?' you ask slightly hurt after all these years of companionship.

'The one you didn't know about' she says... 'The one who never lost his keys!'

Convincing your wife you are still worth knowing is only the first hurdle. There are the harder jobs to do. First you have to tell the girls in the course office that you had your keys all along, so the panic is over, and watch them give the universal body language sign of disapproval, better known as the 'tutting eye roll.' The girls silently spread the message to each other ... We've got a right fruitcake here. Can't even look after his own keys. Then you have to pluck up the courage to tell your fellow 'G' golfers your mistake in all its pathetic glory.

The phone calls come in. Your friends are concerned 'Are you alright professor?' 'Did you manage to sort things out?'

There is a brief moment when you want to tell a little white lie that will make you look and feel much better. You want to invent a story that the crows took them and you are having them all shot. But the moment passes and the spirit of George Washington settles on your conscience. 'Father I cannot tell a lie'. You tell your friends the truth about how pathetic you were and they were in your bag all along. You listen to the laughter on the other end of the phone. With a bit of luck they will forget the incident by next week ... but they do not. You turn up at the next game a bit later to avoid contact and try to disregard their enquiring looks. In the end they can keep the digs in no longer:

'Got your keys professor?' says Big Brother

'Where you going to put them this week?' says the Monarch

'I've got a special compartment for them in my bag' says the Famous Belgian

'Would you like me to look after them for you?' says the Godfather

The Godfather looking after something for you! This really is rubbing insult to injury as most of the time he can't look after something for himself! You finally realize that the ability of 'G' golfers to make cutting remarks is unsurpassed and they will never let you forget. From now on till the bitter end they will wait for the moment to spring the memory lurking in the background, that once upon a time you were a prat, too.

The professor is one of the intellectuals in the group, so it is very surprising when he displays geriatric tendencies. We are glad he does because it gives us all hope. At the end of one particularly showery day we arrived at the club house in our usual analytical mood to total up the scores, discuss the shot of the day and take the piss out of the other hundred or so, when the professor did something rather daft. We had decided to sit outside and were told by another group of golfers to watch out because the seats were wet. The professor in his usual meticulous style got his golfing towel out of his bag, took his time and methodically wiped one of the seats. He returned to his trolley, put the towel back in his bag, came back to the sitting area and sat himself down very uncomfortably in an un-wiped chair.

'Did you see what I just did?' he asked standing up and showing us the stripy wet patches on his trousers and jumper.

'Yes' we said not referring to the fact that we had watched him do it.

'What was that all about?'

'Age related degeneration' we said to appeal to his professorial side.

....

So, readers of these chronicles: Has something similar happened to you, too? Are you willing to admit to senior moments? Please note: This ability to offer your self up for human sacrifice is part of the 'G' golfers' makeup and marks us out as people willing to accept their own inadequacies with good grace and lashings of humour.

And if something like this hasn't happened to you yet, it will. Senior moments will creep up on you as a reminder from the grim reaper that he is waiting down the line and there will definitely be times when:

You are a score card short of a pencil

You're a club shaft short of a grip

Your bag has come off your trolley. (Along with the wheels)
… see below
Your brain has been marked out as 'ground under repair'
Your ability to think has been bashed out of bounds.
It's your round in the bar and you forget.

Whatever you do, enjoy these moments of 'G' golfer gold.

OFF YOUR TROLLEY

One of the classic mind sets in golf is that the game is full of strange moments waiting to happen and one of the incidents that will occur at some stage of your golfing career will, no doubt, involve a trolley. So there you are about to take a master shot towards the hole, as one of your friends shouts 'STOP ….. BEHIND YOU'. No, it's not the cry from the audience in a pantomime, so you stop the flow of your wonderful swing, turn round and see that the trolley you paid so much money for, has developed a life of its own and wandered off. (Or just maybe, you forgot to put the brake on), and what's more, the electric motor is still whirring and accelerating the bloody thing towards the lake.

The whole four ball takes off (well *'takes off'* is too strong a word for geriatric golfers. Perhaps *'creaks into action'* would be better) and makes a beeline for the lake. The race is on. Man versus machine; Mechanical parts versus hip replacement. Karate Kid, the youngest and fittest of us closes the gap with a desperate lunge. But the trolley is faster than any of us and picks up speed down the hill and launches with a wobble into the water, falling on its side and disturbing a moor hen that squawks as if it is laughing at our misfortune. Sparks fly. The engine dies and the owner, who shall remain unidentified, is distraught. At least the reeds on the edge stopped it from becoming a three wheeled submarine.

'What happened there?' the owner asks, realizing it was a stupid question.

The friends stood silently on the bank side and removed their caps as if paying their respects at a funeral before helping retrieve the dead trolley, the dripping bag and the soaking contents by forming a human chain holding on to each other so we, too, do not end up in the watery grave. All for one and one for all.

So … have the wheels ever come off your trolley? I am sure you will have some stories to tell.

Now, where did I leave my car?

'Don't worry, Godfather. You came with me'

An addition to the diary: Some recent and revealing incidents

Just to prove that the 'G' golfing incidents are on-going, I can offer another example of the confusion and physical turmoil often experienced by 'G' golfers that happened this week. (In fact, never a week goes by without some evidence of the inevitable disconnect between brain and game).

It was the fourteenth and the Godfather's turn to drive. He strode purposefully towards the yellow markers, placed his tee in the ground, carefully balanced the ball on top and stepped back to survey the shot in his usual confident style. With great care he settled into his stance and tried a practice swing only to find that what was 'swishing' in his hands was the driver head cover rather than the driver. The Taylor made driver was still nestling in the bag like a discarded toy.

Now, it would have been interesting to see what would have happened if the Godfather had gone through with his driver head shot. (It may even have been better than his normal drive!) But eventually the realization that something was wrong took hold. With a sheepish grin the Godfather stopped, looked at what he was gripping, looked at the driver in his bag and looked at us. 'Stupid pillock' he said in a moment of self-flagellation

Everybody present was inclined to agree, but I bet something like this may have happened to you. If so, it may not be as daft as the example above, but if you have ever taken the wrong club from the bag, not recognized it is the wrong club, gone on to use it, put it back in someone else's bag, chosen the wrong tee, forgot to pick it up, left a club on the fairway, in the bunker or on the green, lost various items of clothing …..

Beware, you are on the slippery slope to 'G' golfing heaven.

………………………………………………………………

It was on the eighteenth when the Godfather launched his ball towards the ditch (Well, I say a ditch, it is in actual fact, more like a tiny channel about two foot wide that drains the fairway into the pond by the tee). After searching for the ball in the trickle of water, the Godfather discovered that it wasn't in the ditch at all but in a difficult lie on the 'other side'. Of course, for a geriatric golfer being on 'the other side' of a small ditch produces a dilemma: Do you back track the forty or so meters to go round via the bridge, or do you attempt 'the jump'?

The Godfather looked at the ditch and decided he could make it. Bearing in mind that it is probably just as easy to step over, this highly tuned athlete took on the psyche of a long jumper, measuring his run up, practicing getting his leg over (an alien concept for a geriatric golfer), before attempting the real thing.

The outcome, you will no doubt have guessed. A comic run up followed by a tenuous wobble on one leg, followed by a half hearted launch, followed by a liquid landing

'O Bugger' the Godfather said, looking a right prat.

'Do it again' we all said.

He didn't respond to our request and took a difficult shot from the rough on 'the other side'. Now, when you are trying <u>not</u> to do something in golf the 'law of inevitability' takes over. And on many occasions, one of us has been heard to mutter, 'Now if I aim for the tree, I am bound to miss it. If I aim to get into the bunker, I am bound to go sailing over it. Or if I try to get into that hazard with my utility club, the Gods will be with me and I'll get clear.' So the

ed this reverse psychology: 'I'm aiming for the
nowing that this was the last thing he wanted. He set
like the true amateur he was. Guess where the ball
at's right: In the ditch. Reverse psychology needed to
be revers

COMPARING AILMENTS, INJURIES AND BRUISED EGOS

One of the problems of being a geriatric golfer is that by definition, there is almost certainly something wrong with you mentally, physically and spiritually! The painful truth is that you can't have reached such advanced years without suffering from the ravages of time and your faults and defects will out. This condition of being prepared for the knackers' yard rears its ugly head as soon as you reach the hallowed ground of the golf club and try to get out of your car and unload the clubs from the back.

After the usual pleasantries of saying hello and commenting on the weather, the conversation inevitably turns to your ailments and how they are progressing. It's like the scene from the film Jaws when Brody, the chief of police, the old seadog captain played by Robert Shaw and the shark expert (Richard Dreyfus) are stuck on a boat in the middle of the ocean and preparing for the horrors ahead. As part of their preparations they try to prove their manhood and increase their credibility by comparing injuries. Only then do they feel adequate enough to go after the shark. As geriatric golfers we seem to follow the same pattern. Declare what's wrong with you first, so people will take pity and then you will be ready to meet the challenge because you've got a good excuse to fail. The conversation in the car park goes something like this:

'How's the shoulder, Monarch of the Glen?' (He had an operation a year ago)

'Not too bad, but the back's playing up.'

'How are the Knees, famous Belgian?' (He's also had several operations)

'Still there, but I hardly got any sleep last night.'

'Surely that's got more to do with the wife?'

'If only!'

'How's the toe, professor?'

'The doctor said there is nothing they can do. It's encapsulitis. His advice was …. If it hurts, just pack up. That's why I might only be playing nine.'

'What did the doctor say, Godfather?'

'Keep taking the tablets.' (The Godfather is on so many tablets, he rattles)

'How about your shoulder, Golf novice?'

'Still can't raise my arm up vertically or to the side, (this lack of capacity is demonstrated), but I can manage to swing'

This contradiction in movements seems a miracle to the others and they grunt as if I must be putting it on. Sometimes I remind them that I did take nine months off because I couldn't even swing without pain. (The result of an old war wound when my humorous was broken near the shoulder). Now I can swing and the any pain I suffer is normally from the quality of the shots.

In fact, the only two people who seem to be problem free are the youngest (The Karate Kid) and probably the eldest (Big Brother)

But there is an unwritten rule in golf which can be expressed by a well known formula: The problems caused by any ailments or injuries are directly proportional to how well we are playing. Put simply: The worse we play, the worse the ailment gets, the better we play the less it affects us. But even if we are playing well, we always put a little reminder in that we still carry a great potential to suffer and we are playing against the odds.

'Not a bad shot, but I did get a little twinge from my back'

'On the green, but I can feel my shoulder coming on'

'I've got to have a camera up my penis tomorrow!'

This last comment usually causes more cringing and screwed up 'agony faces' than all our ailments put together. In fact if you put all our ailments together, the only thing you can be thankful for is that we've got a national health service free at the point of need

This discussion about injuries always gives the geriatric golfer a legitimate excuse for playing like a prat, and it has been known that after a series of bad shots, the pain of the ailment is so strong that some of us have to give up and make our way back to the clubhouse without completing the course. This usually happens on the back nine when all hope is lost, but it has been known on rare occasions on the front nine when the pain of a wayward shot is added to the pain of a wayward back. How much of the pain is psychological and how much genuine, I will leave to the reader to work out, but I bet you've been there too?

However, the time comes for all geriatric golfers when their medical condition has a greater and greater impact on their game right up to the point of no return and the fateful day comes when we will have to pack up. We all want to avoid this but in the end we all know it's got to be somewhere in our futures.

At the moment, this has only affected one of the gang, when the 'Rugby Man' had to hang up his clubs for medical reasons. It is testament to his resilience that he managed to stay with us for so long and we still remember him as a good player and a good friend. He even tried to make a comeback, hired a buggy and concentrated on his short game but it was to no avail. We were so proud of him.

Several of us are under the doctor for long term medical conditions and they too keep playing and 'stay with it', sometimes against all the odds. Perhaps it is an important reminder that we are all bound together by this game called golf come rain or shine. Like musketeers, we go through the pain barrier with each other. It is 'All for one and one for all' as we fight the grim reaper. And if we run out of things to say about ourselves, we can always spread the net to the wives and how they are coping. At least we know that barring a miracle they will not get pregnant!

We are also very inclined to pick up waifs and strays and fellow geriatric golfers who cross out path. Two come to mind: One we will refer to as **'The Ancient One'** in that he seems to ask us or remind us every game how old he is (and he is by far the most ancient). Let's just say he is well into his seventies and an example to us all. Well his age is an example, but sadly not the golf. Renown for the best practice swing you will ever see, followed, when he actually takes his shot, by the crappiest you will ever see, he hangs on in there. Secretly we all hope we will be able to last as long as the ancient one.

Then there's his partner, now to be referred to as the **'Painter and Decorator'**, who still works every now and again and takes great pleasure in picking up top name clubs from car boot sales for bugger all and then showing us how well he can use them, especially when one of us has paid mega bucks for a top club that has been guaranteed to sort out our slice, fat shot, thin shot and general wobbles (Why is it that a new club never does and the more it costs the more it fails? Maybe it's got something to do with the person using it?). The painter and decorator is a smooth operator, and a fair weather golfer who hibernates over winter.

As a geriatric golfer, it also doesn't help to have a fitness suite on the complex as all the bright young things in their multi coloured lycra outfits bounce out of their cars and into intensive work out sessions with an energy level we can barely remember. What's more when they have finished they bounce back with the same level of energy.

Sometimes we hear them speak in the foreign language of fitness fanatics.

'What have you been doing?'

'Extreme Abs Blast'

'I've been doing the SAS circuits.'

'Is that harder than the Navy Seals workout?'

'Yeah. Makes your six pack look even better'

'There's a new class starting next week. It's called the A.A.T.'

'A A T?'

'Yeah, the 'Aerobic Arse Tightening' class to trim up the glutes.

At this point we lose the will to live, wonder whether we have ever had any 'abs' to blast and try to peer over our twelve packs to see if our golf shoes need tying up. This is usually followed by a quick glance at our glutes that are definitely in need of some aerobic arse tightening.

Geriatric golfers do their best to stay fit and healthy but in the end we are part of what will be a sad story. There is no peace in growing old and we have to accept the consequences or as one of us puts it 'Grow old disgracefully'. So what do we old ones have to make up for the absence of 'abs', the inability to touch our toes and the inherent flexibility of an iron bar? We have to use the wealth of experience that only comes with age. We certainly have enough experience to predict that if we ever turned up in the fitness suite for a bit of arse tightening, we would never leave alive.

We also watch as the single guys in the pro shop eye up the young shapely females on their way through to the fitness area and realize that's what we probably did once in the dim and distant past. In fact in our day, that's all we could do... just watch. The swinging sixties was a myth for most of us. *'Look but don't touch'* was part of our generations experience and now we have reached the era of anything goes, whatever we had has already gone. In fact, we only have enough strength to display the green eyed monster of jealousy. If only we were part of generation X …. What would we do? Of course, Monarch of the Glen still thinks he is in with a chance with the bright young things and we sometimes catch him drooling over his score card.

As we sit in the sunshine at the club house, on a warm summers day, the ancient one has also developed the habit of going extremely quiet (as do we all?), when any of the female trainers from the gym go by. They all wear 'T' shirts with the logo 'here to help' emblazoned on the front and back. One infamous day the ancient one could hold back the beast no longer and yelled at the top of his voice. 'You can help me out any time you like, darling.'

He was immediately disowned. We did no know which way to look. Fortunately the young lady kept walking.

Help me up, someone

HEARING AIDS AND OTHER ARTIFICIAL BODY PARTS

There comes a time in every geriatric golfer's life when he needs help to do the basics, and we are not talking here about grip, ball position and posture but things like walking, talking, bending, eating, breathing, listening, peeing and generally all the functions that show you are still in the land of the living! There is also no doubt that the day will come when your faculties begin to fail to such an extent that you might have to rely on artificial aids to keep you going. Examples of this downward spiral to disability and the use of prosthetics are many and varied.

1. As you greet your fellow golfers in the car park, you have a sudden panic attack: … Did I put my teeth in today? If the answer is 'NO', your first up response is to try to talk with your mouth closed. Not only does this make you sound like an idiot, but because of your restricted facial expression, they gain the impression that you are in a bad mood and not worth talking to anyway. This embarrassment is sometimes tempered by the fact that your fellow golfers have also failed to put in their collection of pearly whites. This lack of the proper number of teeth becomes especially apparent when you sit opposite each other in the bar after the round exchanging stories about the game and notice the gaps. Forgetting your teeth may also be associated with the fact that you are losing the ability to remember anything and everything anyway, in which case you are in deeper trouble because you might also forget your clubs, your name and the names of your fellow golfers. This can be a regular occurrence for G golfers … what's your name again?

Even when you have remembered to put your teeth in, you may not have used any or enough denture paste, which can result in you spitting your teeth out as a result of shouting loudly when you have managed to play a good shot, or uttering an expletive after a bad shot. It is also possible that you can leave your teeth implanted in a snack bar when you take a comfort break and pull them out while still attached. The other problem is that a piece of nut or sweet becomes lodged under the plate. You then have a choice of finding an opportune moment to take the dentures out to give them a clean, (not any easy things to do when you are trying to avoid slow play), or putting up with oral irritation for the rest of the round.

2. It is hard enough to communicate on a golf course with the distances involved and the odd howling gale that makes words disappear into oblivion. Spare a thought then for the golfer who is becoming hard of hearing. The Godfather was the first of our outfit to need artificial amplification on both ears. We didn't really know he had a problem until he turned up one day with some little flesh coloured implants behind his lobes and wires that seemed to connect to his brain. This made him look the bionic man. It works fine until you try talking to him when he has his back towards you and everything you say meets the proverbial brick wall.

So there he is on the tee and very impolitely we are discussing the situation is Syria (as you do in your *geriatric golfers can change the world* mode) and exchanging details of Islam that seems to be at the heart of the troubles. 'It's either the Sunnis or the Shias' says the professor, always up with the times. 'Sunnis believe that the son of Mohammed is the true leader; Shias think it is his cousin… or something like that. Anyway Sunnis are one tribe and Shias the other.'

The godfather turned round wanting to join in our riveting conversation. 'What are you talking about **Sonny** and **Cher** for?' he said remembering the famous singing duo and bursting into a verse of 'I've got you babe! … I got you to hold my hand, I got you to understand'

'No ... No' said the professor ... 'Sunnis and Shias!'

The Godfather grunted and clearly did not understand this had become a joke.

Apart from collapsing with laughter at the mistranslation and the standard of the singing, we realised that the Godfathers hearing aids don't work when you are behind him. To enable better communication in future we resolved to keep in front of him, mouth our words more clearly as if he is a foreigner and learn sign language.

3. I also have to admit to losing the plot in the hearing stakes: Big brother had shanked an approach shot into a ditch. From a distance away he shouted something to me which sounded like 'did you see my ball?'

'It's in the ditch' I yelled back trying to be helpful.

 Big brother begins to march towards me with a sterner face ... 'Did you see my ball?'

I cup my hands to my mouth to project my voice ... 'It's in the ditch.'

The gap was closing fast. Once more the exchange took the same pattern ... (Did you see my ball? / It's in the ditch) and still Big brother was marching towards me even more angry.

Of course what he was really saying was 'Have you got a ball retriever?' which is so far away from my translation, that it makes it comparable to trying to communicate in serbo-croat and mandarin

I only understood the true meaning of what he was saying when he had just about reached me but the question had changed ... 'I know my ball is in the bloody ditch, ... I was asking if you have got a ball retriever!'

'Oh' I said finally enlightened ... 'you were asking if I've got a ball retriever ... No I Sorry!'

Needless to say he was not impressed, turned round and took the long walk back to the ditch to take a drop.

THE STRANGE CASE OF THE CREAKING SHOE

We have lately recruited a new member to out 'G' golfer group who will for the purposes of these chronicles be called Sergeant Sergeant (or SS for short). As an ex royal marine who won the Falklands war singlehandedly, he had seen better days and suffers from a bad shoulder, hip, knee and just about every other joint in his body. He is also left handed which, to us righties seems like the worst handicap of all (We have enough trouble using the proper side.)

A round with SS is always interesting but because of his ailments is always a bit on the slow side. He also developed a critical condition called 'creaking shoe'. This will remain a vivid memory and one of the highlight of our time on the course. We first discovered it when he was on the tee. A laboured backswing produced this awful creaking sound as if a cat was being strangled. After a pause this was followed by a further creak on the downswing that sounded as if he was passing wind.

At first we thought it was the shoulder joint in need of a bit of WD40, but it ended up being the left shoe. From then on we could not escape. Every tee shot produced the same combination of sounds … (strangled cat on the upswing and an extended wispy fart on the downswing). I pointed this out to the professor who listened with me to make sure it was not a figment of my imagination. He confirmed it was a bad case of creaking shoe. Needless to say, even though we tried hard, every time SS tee'd up, we could not contain the laughter. (And the more we tried to bottle it up the worse it got.) Our problem escalated. SS would take to the tee and even before he got there we would react in a very infantile way … basically crying, collapsing, talking gibberish, trying not to look and holding our hands tight over our ears. Unfortunately strangled cat and wispy fart continued to penetrate the barriers. Although this is no doubt un-gentlemanly conduct, it could not be helped. There is nothing more pathetic than the sight of 'G' golfers out of control. Bye the way, because of the hearing aids, the godfather still thinks that SS is passing wind on the follow through.

SS has now gone to Australia for four weeks and we are in remission. We await his return with interest and it means we have 28 days to learn how to cope. If he turns up with the same shoes … we will be in big trouble with the near certainty of being banned from the course.

Other signs of not coping include:
* Hiring a buggy because you can't make it round on two legs
* The prolific use of pain relieving gels and pads that make you smell like a chemical factory. (When you reach the incontinent stage it really is a bummer!)

THE ROUND THAT GAVE YOU A NOSE BLEED!

We all have our target and goals and achieving them, usually against the odds, gives you a real buzz. I am pleased to say that over three years I have seen my target reduce from trying to reach a 100 to getting under a 100, to getting in the mid 90's and with some application, these have been consistently achieved. But then the question arises: What do you do now? How do you get under 90? And how do you hit the magic number of 80?

You scrutinize your game. Maybe it's the putting, maybe it's the short game, maybe it's making sure you hit fairways. Maybe it's pure luck. Reality says this feat of scoring is beyond you, but then the day comes when it's within your reach.

It was a fair weather Monday (not our usual golfing day) and the godfather and big brother invited me to join them. In the competitive thrust of 'G' golfing folklore this day will go down in the *anals*! The round started off with a wobble into the trees, but some nifty shots rescued a par five. Then the round began to build into alien territory as if you were walking on thin ice. Par followed par until the novice completed the front nine in 37 losing only one shot on the most difficult hole on the course

'This is getting boring' said Big Brother as we walked on to the back nine. He had already given up scoring in disgust.

'Makes you want to pack up now' said the novice not wishing to push his luck. 'In fact the score is so good, I think I might be getting a nose bleed!'

Big Brother looked at the novice with that glint in his eye. 'It can be arranged' he said thumping his right hand into his gloved palm. If you are in the lead, rub it in. Big Brother and the Godfather watched the novice ace the next three holes in a par, a birdy and a par. It was the thirteenth. The novice was evens and Big Brother wanted to 'get even'!

Apart from a few blips on the tricky 15th, the novice recorded a final score of 78 finishing with two well- constructed pars. The lifetime ambition to get below 80 was achieved.

Whether it will ever happen again remains to be seen but the novice can now die happy and shuffle off to the great golf course in the sky with a smile on his face. The score card will be framed, put in a prominent position and brought out every time the boys come around.

THE DAY THE GODFATHER DEFIED THE LAWS OF PHYSICS AND BIOLOGY

Picture the scene: A sunny day in June, the birds singing, the geriatric golfers discussing the finer details of course management, but the godfather's eyesight or mental state causing problems.

'Look at those pheasants' he said pointing to a collection of birds by the lake who were basking in the long grass

We all turned towards where he was pointing and looked at each other a bit mystified. Were we missing something? 'Pheasants?' we asked politely.

'Yes, pheasants.' He said a bit more exasperated. 'Right in front of you.'

Now, those of you who know your birds will realize that male pheasants are brightly coloured birds with magnificent feathers and plumage and the females are more of a dingy brown. In front of us were these wading birds with webbed feet, green heads and yellow bills, who were quacking.

'They are ducks' we suggested.

'No pheasants' said the Godfather sticking to his guns.

'But they're clucking like ducks, Godfather.'

'Yes, they're pheasants'

Big Brother then used that world famous expression. 'If you looks like a duck, quacks like a duck, and swims like a duck, it must be a ruddy duck.'

The Godfather looked again at the gathering of birds and a pained expression slowly spread across his face (even more pained than when he misses a putt.) 'Shit' he said finally realizing his mistake 'They're ducks'. Of course he tried to make out it was a deliberate mistake and he was testing us out, but we were having none of it.

'Think I don't know what a duck looks like?' he asked trying to cover his tracks.

'Yes' we replied in unison.

Every now and again we return to mocking mode, as befits all geriatric golfers the world over, and re-live this moment of humiliation by asking him as we go round the course what the birds are. I am happy to say his eyesight, mental capacity and awareness has improved, which is more than we can say for the golf.

....

It was on the seventeenth that the mystery unfolded. The godfather was on the tee and looking as good as can be expected. He had been driving well and the confidence he needed (which is sometimes in short supply) was high. He set himself, ready to perform his most effective drive of the day. His back swing was unusual, the sound of the strike peculiar, his follow through awkward and we all looked down the fairway to track the ball.

But the ball was nowhere to be seen. 'Where did that go?' he asked

We had time to shake our heads, peer into the distance and look at each other. Suddenly the ball landed on the Godfather's head. Instead of all his effort being converted into the normal trajectory of a drive that sent the ball arching forward maybe two hundred yards, it had somehow sent the ball up vertically and with a significant delay (it must have reached a fair height) had landed with a thump on his cap.

It must be noted here that this speciality shot from the Godfather has been repeated on several occasions, so it is no fluke. We have not worked out how he does it and may call in a scientist working on the 'God' particle for further advice. It may well be that the Godfather has discovered some secret force unknown to man that could change the course of history.

The laws of physics say that to every action there is an equal and opposite reaction, force equals mass times acceleration and that energy cannot be created or destroyed. On this occasion the Godfather had somehow destroyed these fundamental laws and turned himself into the GOD we all knew he could be with dominion over the laws of nature. In the future he may even have a particle named after him.

Since this spectacular example of a hit that wasn't a hit, there has been an advert on TV starring Rory Mcilroy, the open champion. The advert places him with a bad lie in a bunker. To everybody's amazement he faces the wrong way, away from the green and back down the fairway. He prepares to hit the ball with the same concentration as the Godfather displayed and with a miraculous shot he spins the ball so it rises into the air, travels back down the fairway and then spins backwards over his head towards the hole. It is good to note that one of our geriatric golfers and Rory, the superstar of golf can both defy the laws of physics. It is an honour that we can mention them in the same sentence and in the same breath.

The Godfather is known for producing other miracle shots (i.e. near on impossible) that don't always help his game. He frequently hits the tee a further distance than the ball, is often taking his second shot from the ladies tee and loses more tees than any other human being on the planet. In fact when he is playing, shares in plastics companies on the stock market rise.

He also has more 'Mulligans' than anyone else.

For the uninitiated a 'Mulligan' is a free shot allowed when you really make a pigs' ear of your drive. I've not been allowed one yet, but if we are in benevolent mood and one of our fellow geriatric golfers is playing so badly that he is becoming suicidal, we often call 'A Mulligan'.

The Karate Kid introduced us to it when the Professor and the Monarch of the Glen were having a bad day. It is obviously completely illegal and rarely applied. Big Brother has claimed one when one of the G golfers (who shall remain nameless) was talking while Big Brother was executing a drive. Executing is the right word as the ball departed from this life to the next. Big Brothers' stare can also kill from twenty paces so another attempt and a Mulligan was allowed without question. (This one, too went into never - never land) I don't know where the term 'Mulligan' comes from, whether anybody else uses it, or why it is called a 'Mulligan.'

Maybe one of our readers will know.

GET YOUR DONNAYS OUT!

As a novice golfer, it is interesting how you are slowly exposed to the vocabulary, terminology and etiquette of golf. I am sure that each set of geriatric golfers develop their own code words and language to describe what happens. Here are a few of ours. I hope they will be of interest. Maybe you could share your own or as you go round the course, adopt some of ours:

'Get your Donnays out'

I first heard this as an expression from the professor. At first I thought he was being suggestive and slightly rude and that to be initiated into the world of golf you had to expose yourself somewhere down the ninth fairway. I now know it is an expression he, and now everyone else uses when they are playing badly and losing lots of balls. Apparently 'Donnays' are budget golf balls that cost very little and are not too painful to lose. It is one of the certainties of 'sod's law' that if you do get one of your expensive balls out you are bound to lose it early in its life or even on the first hit. It is, therefore, much better to use a budget ball, especially in the early part of the round when you are still getting your eye in.

There also seems to be a view amongst geriatric golfers that the more expensive the balls or the equipment you use, the better you will play and that the greater cost will somehow make up for any defects in your play. This is, of course, not true at our level of play, but paying an extra few quid for a ball will conjure up the illusion that you are a professional and deserving of the best. This feeling persists until the special ProV1 super-dimpled, max fly, huge distance, minimal deviation ball you thought would cure your slice spins out of control and is lost forever until it is sold back to you as a special refurbished ball.

And what a wonderful business model that is: Buy a ball .... Lose it ..... Find it .... Wash it .... Put a little stamp on it ..... Sell it back to a cost conscious golfer at half the price .... Lose it again etc.

It must also be stated here while we are dealing with economic issues that the professor is an expert on re-cycling and in the economics of golf. Born at the end of the second world war he was badly scared by the austerity of that time, the rationing and the make do and mend attitude that deprived him of treats and sweets when he was young. He will, therefore not spend a penny when a half penny will do. (Not that this item of currency exists any longer in Britain). He will, therefore rescue any items of equipment cast away into the bins on the golf course ready for refurbishment. Of special note is his ability to revitalize discarded trolleys and inside out umbrellas that have been mutilated by the wind.

He is also an expert golf ball finder and, rumor has it, has not actually paid for a golf ball in the last decade.

A Sally Gunnell.

Monarch of the Glen uses this expression when anyone tops the ball and instead of it rising majestically into the air, it bounces in fits and starts along the ground to its final resting place usually nowhere near where it was meant to be. Sally Gunnell was a British runner who won Olympic gold in the 400 meter hurdles and in similar fashion a 'Sally Gunnell' golf shot runs along the ground, jumping up every now and again but doesn't go very far.

The professor has alternative definition of a 'Sally Gunnell' that is much more cruel. He defines it as 'a shot that is ugly but keeps on running'. How dare he refer to the golden girl of British Athletics in this way?

This shot is not to be confused with a **Barnes Wallis**, which goes further and bounces higher as well as running. Barnes Wallis was the inventers of the bouncing bomb that the Dam-busters used in the second world war. (And most of our gang remember the second world war and rationing). They were launched at low level to bounce like a spinning pebble over water before demolishing German dams. This shot often happens when you are trying to get over a bunker and ends up with you in it.

An 'Adolf'   Two shots and you are still in the bunker

Shitenhausen

To continue the German theme, this expression is often used by the Godfather after a particularly bad shot (especially a putt) where he adopts the body language of an irate penguin, flaps round in circles, simulates the banging of his club into the turf and shouts 'Shitenhausen'. I have no idea whether this is a real German word but the use of it helps the Godfather to relieve his built up frustration. If he was not able to explode in this way, we fear he would either self combust on the fairway or attack another 'G' golfer.

Similar expressions such as 'Burger King' 'Bollocks' 'Pratt face' and 'What a dick head' 'Pathetic' or 'Oh goodness' perform the same psychological function

'There May be Trouble Ahead' *

Taken from the Fred Astaire song 'Let's face the music and dance', this is often sung on the way to an unknown lie either in the woods, by a lake or in the rough. The famous Belgian was the originator of this idea. We normally only sing the first verse but the golf muse has inspired me to try to invent some more. With apologies to a once beautiful song, it goes like this:

There maybe trouble ahead
And as I can't see the ball
What's the chance?
Let's face a bogie and dance.

And now I've seen where lies
There is no hope I can hit it,
'I'll miss it', I cry
Let's face double bogie and dance.

(Main song/ tune change)

Swing, Why don't you swing your wood
Take a divot where you just stood
And then .....

There maybe trouble ahead.
And as I can't see the ball
What's the chance?
It's now triple bogie ... no dance, dance

It's now triple bogie .. no dance

Please note: Anybody who knows this song or was around when it was first released is definitely a geriatric golfer.

Better make allowances For the Wind.

Yes, you guessed it. This wind is not the meteorological variety but the one produced at frequent intervals by Monarch of the Glenn and on the odd occasion by the Godfather when he is straining too much on a long drive. We have no understanding of why this condition emanates from the Monarch, but it may have something to do with his diet or a traumatic experience in his childhood.

It is often said that good friends have the comfort of being able to fart in each others company without embarrassment. All we can say is that Monarch of the Glen puts this theory to the test so much that we must be really, really good friends.

Although many of us would admit to the silent variety (or at least an attempt to keep it silent), Monarch of the Glen only passes wind on the scale of loud to very loud and long lasting and very very long lasting. All of them are deadly and we think this can only be part of his tactic to put us off our game. On a bad day we will make allowances for the wind before he takes every drive. On an even worse day, he will feel the need to become windy as you are taking a shot.

But make allowances for the wind we do. And we would not be without him.

The eagle has landed

This term has only been used on the fourteenth hole and brings back the memory of the professor getting the one and only eagle in the history of our group. He hit a good drive. The second shot (some 110 yards at least) sailed over a small rise at the start of the green that obscures the view and then out of sight. As we made our way to the green the professor was concerned about what had happened to his ball. Had it gone through? Had it disappeared? The answer became clear. It had ended up in the hole. The eagle had landed but nobody knew. To this day when we are playing with the professor and reach the fourteenth, we pay homage to his skill (or perhaps his good fortune). It is a landmark in the hall of fame.

Too many Weetabix / Not enough Weetabix

These terms are used depending on the strength of the shot. If it runs too far, you have had too many of this delicious breakfast cereal. If it's too short, you have not had enough.

I Hit the Grund

An expression made famous by the famous Belgian who although having excellent English (as well as three other languages) mispronounces the word 'ground', turning it into a more earthy 'GRUND'. Whenever one of our group take more earth than ball, this is the expression we use. 'I hit the grund.' This is sometimes preceded by 'Oh bollocks!' or followed by 'what a dick head'

The famous Belgian's language skills are legendary, but every now and again, much to our amusement, he mispronounces well know English phrases or sayings. For example: When he ends up in trouble after a particularly crap shot, his favourite saying is …. Oh No. I'm up the CREEP, (instead of up the Creek). Sometimes he adds to this and the expression becomes . 'Oh no. I'm up the creep without a piddle' and he once referred to the paralympics as the *'paraplegics.'*

When reaching the eighteenth tee the Famous Belgian's accent has also morphed the word 'Last hole' into 'L'arsole'. To complete the full sentence he normally uses goes something like this: 'Well boys, we 'ave reached de L' Arse hole.' The first time he said it, I must admit turning round to see if someone was reaching for my rear end but now the phrase just raises a smile.

He has also been heard to say 'Ere we are again. Ze l'arse - ole chaps'. I believe there is an ointment you can get for this!

However, it is true to say that the famous Belgian is not alone in losing the ability to express him self. One of the characteristics of growing old is that you lose words in what are euphemistically called 'senior moment.' Unfortunately, one of the hallmarks of a geriatric golfer is that not only when do they words lose but when they them find talk they frequently gibberish!

And if you had trouble reading that last sentence: *'I'm not so think as you drunk I am'*

'That's enough torture for one day'

Maybe anyone who plays golf has to have a masochistic or sadistic streak somewhere inside them to keep going back! Especially, when they are learning how to play or suffering from the ravages of time. Why else would you keep turning up for your weekly session of ritual humiliation?

'Where are you off to dear?' says the wife

'I'm off to the prison of doom to see my dominatrix.' You say as you put your clubs (the instruments of your self inflicted torture) into the boot.

'Looks like you're playing golf to me'

'Does it?' you reply 'I thought they were the same thing.'

And when you look at the fundamentals of this addiction, there is something very strange about turning up to get to get a weekly fix of failure, frustration and self loathing in between the odd flushes of success. There is no doubt about it, this game will make you feel inadequate, chastised, useless as a man, whipped within an inch of your life and dominated by the elements. Maybe that's why we love it so much.

'I always thought there was something wrong with you' she says without a sign of pity.

So, this expression 'That's enough torture for one day' relates to the above analysis of being psychologically disturbed. It is frequently used by 'G' golfers as they finish another crap round and move morbidly into the club house to drown their sorrows in the bar to discuss the 'shots they left on the course'. However, as there are so many of these 'lost 'shots , no one can remember them and there is not enough time to discuss them anyway, so drowning sorrows seems like a much better idea.

This expression: 'That's enough torture for one day' is also used as you walk dejected from the driving range as yet another attempt to sort out a problem with your game bites the dust. And even if you do manage to 'improve' the swing, sort the slice, beautify the bunker play or get more positive with the pitching, by the time you pat yourself on the back for your momentary success, you have picked up another bad habit that makes your game even worse. In this sense playing golf is a bit like being on a merry go round or rearranging the deckchairs on the Titanic. But still, like the Celine Dion song applied to all geriatric golfers, everywhere: Even though your ship is sinking, 'Your heart must go on' … which reminds me of a song. (Oh no, please not again, I hear you saying so I apologize before I start). Sung to the tune from Titanic:

Sometimes on the golf course
I know I am rubbish
But I know the game must go ooooon

Yet another bogie
Is marked on my score card
But they tell me
I must go ooooon

Near, far
Wherever you are
I must search for my ball
But its go-oo-ne

(Musical interlude of haunting pipes)

Now that I have found it
I aim for the last hole
Once again the game it goes ooooon

Right until the moment
And the end of my story
When the game,
It cannot go ooooon

Time stops
The golf ball, it drops
And then only the memories
Go ooooon

(Crescendo of haunting pipes till the end)

By the time you have tried singing this, you will definitely become aware of the expression: *'That's enough torture for one day.'*

In this chapter you have read about a few of our golfing expressions. Why not borrow some to try out on your gang of 'G' Golfers. Or maybe you have some of your own you would like to share?

Why not write them below:

DANGEROUS PLAY?

You might guess that as most geriatric golfers are unpredictable, there are times when we have to run for cover from wayward shots that go anywhere but where they were supposed to …. And you would be right. In fact, the unwritten rule of staying behind the hitter when they are taking their shots has, quite literally, been a life saver. But there are times when we stray from this golden path of righteousness and move unconsciously into harms way.

One of the first incidents I saw was when Monarch of the Glen was about to hit his drive from the first tee. His set up, as always, was a picture of magnificence. Ball to the front of his stance, eyes on the ball, fag in mouth, deep breath …. Bang. (Monarch had the sort of driver that gave out a sort of tinny explosive sound that you could hear from all over the golf course). But instead of the ball accelerating into the distance, he shanked it and sent it directly sideways.

Dangerous moments always seem to manifest themselves in slow motion, as if you are seeing your life pass before you. So it was on this occasion as the ball spun at ninety degrees to the fairway and thudded into the professor's shoulder as he was standing a few yards to the side. Luckily the speed of such a crap shot was not great and the professor took the hit like a man. Everyone except the Monarch checked that the victim was still breathing and despite a shocked look on his face, the professor was okay. However, the reaction of the Monarch was more on his next shot than the near death experience of his fellow golfer. With the calmness of a psychotic killer with an empathy bypass, the Monarch ignored the professor, made no eye contact, showed no concern, issued no apology, and walked calmly to retrieve the offending ball laying at the professor's feet. His next shot was spectacularly successful.

I have noticed ever since that when the Monarch is on the tee, especially the first tee, the rest of the G golfers take extra care to make sure they are behind him. The only problem with this, of course, is if he decides to pass wind. As you can imagine, this is a good example of double jeopardy.

I wouldn't play with that lot
If I were you

On reflection, the Monarch seems to figure as the central character in this chapter on danger. Maybe danger follows him around.

It was on the twelfth. This is a hole that doglegs to the left over some tall conifers and frequently destroys those golfers who have a natural slice or cannot draw a ball. (This means most of us). The godfather had sent his ball into the woods as if magnetized by trouble. We eventually found it some twelve feet behind a large tree that restricted the shot back to the fairway. The Monarch for some reason attempted to hide behind this tree so only the fag in his mouth was showing on the right hand side.

'It will give you something to aim at' he said as the cigarette jiggled up and down and he puffed smoke into the air.

Some of us thought this looked a bit dangerous as ping pong among the trees was a regular feature of our game.

Give you something to aim at.

The godfather took aim, presumably to avoid the tree (and therefore the person hiding behind it) and went for a full shot. The ball struck the tree trunk full on, about head height and pinged straight back. One shudders to think what would have happened if the Monarch had moved, but his nerve held even though he was directly in the line of fire. Now, the Monarch is a retired RAF technician, but to put him self in harms way behind the tree was surely above and beyond the call of duty, some would say, even stupid. This day, because of The Monarch's dice with death has since become known as 'The round of living dangerously.'

The inherent dangers of playing golf: Mental illness!

As a behavioural psychologist, I am very interested in observing human behaviour and, with tongue in cheek, would like to put forward the theory that all golfers, especially those of more advanced years, have an increased chance of becoming mentally ill.

Studies are only just beginning into the causes of golf induced mental instability but early indications show that it may be caused by the brains natural reaction to stress and how humans cope with failure. The stress on a golf course is far less than on a battlefield, but constant exposure over a long period of time (sometimes called 'Tee fatigue') can result in post traumatic stress disorders where flash backs of particularly bad shots take over your life. The Godfather has even been known to walk down the street practicing the shots that went wrong and there have been reported sightings of him practicing thrusting his hips at the local supermarket. It's a bit like a nightmare version of Groundhog Day when you relive your worst ever round and cannot escape until love releases you! As some 'G' golfers have been playing all their lives, they are particularly at risk of the drip feed of stress which can have the same effect as Chinese water torture.

Prolonged bouts of failure can also lead to a downward spiral of self esteem where you start from thinking you are crap to the next stage of feeling like you are crap to the more advanced stage of knowing you are crap, and to add insult to injury, as you grow even older, things are likely to get worse. For example: The Godfather has kept all his score cards going back maybe twelve years. (This is another indicator of obsessive compulsive disorder). When asked what has happened to his scores over the last twelve years, without hesitation he says

'Well, they've got worse, but they were pretty bad back then!'

Most 'G' golfers are brought up in the school of hard knocks and in the end get used to the fact that they have 'peaked'

The evidence mentally challenged behaviour is all around you on the golf course. Tell me if you have witnessed the following either in yourself or others: Apoplectic fits accompanied by intense bouts of swearing and foaming at the mouth. Cries of anguish from adjacent fairways that lead you to believe the trolls are coming. Psychotic delusions of grandeur as you set up for a shot and believe that you really are Tiger Woods (although you have never crashed a four by four running away from your wife!); Obsessive behaviour where, when you make a bad shot, you keep doing the same thing over and over again just to prove your coach was wrong and you are right; Depressive mood swings where you wander round in circles looking for your ball in the rough, blaming the world for your troubles. Bi Polar disorder (Manic Depressive) where in the space of one hole you can be on cloud nine with a magnificent shot one moment and wanting to bury yourself on the fairway the next;

**Manic Depressive buried here
with his balls**

More evidence of mental illness on the golf course

The Schizophrenic condition of hearing voices in your head telling you to 'relax', 'swing with your body', aim down the line of power' and other similar mantras that cause you to forget who you are and where you are and enter that state of mind called 'golf trance'; The more dangerous voices in your head telling you to 'kill' if anyone should speak while you are on the tee. Paranoid thoughts that everything is plotting against you and preventing you from making a decent score: the birds singing to deliberately put you off, the noises that come up from the cracks in the ground that mock you, the wind that bends your shot away from target, the trees that move, as if they are CGI extras in 'Lord of the Rings' to block a wonderful drive. It is a conspiracy and even the Gods are against you. In fact in bad cases of golf induced schizophrenia, golfers suffer from chronic hallucinations, the most common of which is that they see themselves winning the open and putting on the green jacket. How much more crackpot could you get? Some eminent psychiatrists also believe that some 'G' golfers would have a better round if they took LSD!

Physical manifestations of this inner turmoil include twitching, ticking, obscene utterances as if you are suffering from tourettes, the holding of your head in your hands, shaking, beating the ground and the emission of strange noises.

I knew you would recognize these descriptions and symptoms. They can be found on golf courses all over the world. But don't get too concerned. The clinical psychologists have identified this as a common condition and are working on a pill that deals with the mental wobbles of golfers and with one swallow this miracle pill will turn you into better players. Apparently it is closely related to that other drug used by elderly males. (And if you hadn't guessed already, it's Viagra).

However, they are looking for a name for this wonder pill. Please write any suggestions below.

Suggestions collected so far include: 'Zinger', 'Swinger'; 'In the hole' (for the American market); 'Chip 'n Pin'; 'Par None'. They will also be looking for someone to write the advertising campaign slogans and TV commercials. What an exciting opportunity!

All you need to do is create a story board. I can see it now: A 'G' golfer struggling to hit the ball; A doctor in a white coat comes up and offers him a 'Zinger' from a customized package. 'This pill will change your life' he says; The golfer takes it, suddenly turns into Lee Westwood and creams a shot onto the green within two feet of the flag; The actor playing Lee Westwood (or the real Lee Westwood if the budget can afford it) turns to the camera 'The Zinger Pill, 100 % guaranteed to lower your score' he says with a CGI twinkle on one of his teeth.

Of course this ad would never get through the Advertising Standards Authority but geriatric golfers will definitely remember the days when smoking ads were allowed on TV and the enormous impact of the Hamlet ad, with the golfer trapped in the bunker for life taking shot after shot to get out. Eventually he accepts his fate and smokes a hamlet cigar in recognition he will never escape as the air on a 'G' string plays in the background.

Many 'G' golfers are able to say ...... 'I was that man'

An example of probable mental illness

It was somewhere on the back nine where the well known psychotic condition of 'golf rage' took over. We were in a four ball with an elderly couple in a buggy (elderly, even by our standards) coming up rapidly behind us. Apparently they had asked several times to play through but according to the rules as our senior members understood them, this was not compulsory. Now, when the Monarch is not playing well, his ability to deal with pressure evaporates. The gentleman in the couple tempted fate a few times by taking an early shot and sending it close to our position. The Monarch's temperature gauge began to rise and it was now close to boiling point and you could hear him chuntering. For the Monarch, this is a sure sign that the red mist was descending.

Once again an early shot from the elderly gent behind trickled past us. It was the straw that broke the camels back or, more appropriately, the shot that shattered the chandelier. The Monarch picked up the elderly gentleman's ball, threw it back at him and began a club - waving, full frontal charge towards where he was standing.

' ****ing do that again and I'll break your ****ing club over your head' said the Monarch, a statement, which in basic form, is so far outside the etiquette of golf parlance that it comes from another planet. Although no one heard the exact words, the Monarch also denigrated the elderly gentleman's country of origin by saying something that ended with the well know phrase 'You Scottish Bastard'

Now, when you know the Monarch as well as we do, you make allowances that sometimes he does come from another planet. He can be scary when he is 'in one' but you have just got to stand your ground and the pressure fades away into comedy. When you don't know him and he goes into 'golf rage', it is probable that you may be scarred for life and open to the symptoms of post traumatic stress disorder. (Flash backs, psycho-somatic palpitations and nightmares). The elderly couple behind us turned white and began to shake, retreating to their buggy for protection and a quick get away.

The Karate Kid stepped into the breach and with his zen like mediation skills, became the peacemaker with the result that the elderly couple regained their composure and moved to the next hole to get in front and away from this nasty man.

Apparently they did complain at the club house that some madman had threatened them but nothing became of it and the Monarch was left alone to play another day.

And on one of those other days, I suffered a similar fate to the elderly couple. It was on the tenth, the wind was behind and I hit one of my better drives which landed well away from the Monarch but trickled past him. It was such a long drive and so far away, no one on the tee had the slightest idea that it had reached the group in front. Even Big Brother with his 'X' ray vision had not seen a problem. We certainly did not know that with a certain degree of venom, the Monarch had lost the plot, taken a club and belted the ball back a further thirty yards with the accompaniment of a few well chosen swear words.

'But he's a mate' said the Godfather who was playing with him

'So what?' replied Monarch of the Glen.

The moral to this story: If the Monarch is in front, take more care (unless you consciously want to wind him up!)

....

It was on the first tee when I got the shock of my life. I shaped up for a drive and it was a nice one. I paused to admire my handy work (a rare occurrence on the first tee), not realizing that the Monarch was standing close behind me holding his driver tight and anxious to get on with his shot.

I stepped back to pick up my tee, bent down and felt the hot metal of the Monarch's drive shaft attempting to penetrate my back passage!

He did not feel the need to move, but I did.

'Just as well it wasn't the other end' he said with a big smile on his face.

Needless to say, ever since this episode of unrequited love, we have been the best of friends.

....

Over two years of playing golf, I have only seen one potentially really dangerous moment. This was on the twelfth. The Karate Kid had sent his ball into the woods to the left, rapidly followed by the professor, whose ball did not go in as far. Because of the location of their balls and the configuration of the trees they were not able to see each other. The Karate Kid played a nice shot out and began to emerge from the wood in front of the professor. The professor was about to take a full swing. Once again slow motion came into play. We tried to shout 'stop' but it was too late. The professor creamed a beautiful shot. It flew past the Karate Kid at head height. Luckily the Gods were with us, but the margin for error was very small.

Moral: It is important to remember safety at all times. I am sure that readers of this diary will have their own comic and not so comic examples of accidental dangerous play.

GOLF LESSONS: A STEEP LEARNING CURVE WITH PLENTY OF DIPS, SLIPS AND YIPPS

We can all reflect on how we learned, and still learn to play this wonderful game of golf and where it all went wrong (or right).... And I am sure we all have stories about methods that worked for us or tips that didn't. As a non golf playing Physical Education teacher my view of the game was always naïve to say the least. When I saw professional golf on TV it looked so easy. The effortless swing of the ladies, the dead eye precision of the putts, the sight of the ball sailing away into the distance made it all look so simple. All you had to do was hit the ball and aerodynamics would do the rest. I had no bearing on the skill involved. What the TV stations ought to do is to show amateur golfers like us struggling to come to terms with their inadequacies. Something tells me that in its own way this would be just as entertaining as watching the professionals, and classy commentators like Peter Allis and Ken Brown would have a field day. I can hear them now:

'Yes, it's the Godfather on the tee. Note the particular way he shakes with his own unique style.'

'As the Famous Belgian shapes up for this shot, I want you to try to work out where he is aiming.'

'The professor really does look the part until it's his turn'

'Ken is on the tenth green. What do you think, Ken?'

'Big Brother obviously misread the green. He didn't realize it was there.'

Anyway, working out how you are going to develop as a player is a personal journey without end. Taking lessons pretty soon after my first attempt to hold a club is my first memory of this journey. 'If you are serious … pay for it' and in the end I am glad I did (not that I knew it at the time)

The golf professional at Lakeside Lodge, now to be known as *'Handy Andy'* was booked to give me six basic lessons with the starting proviso that 'I knew nothing.' Handy Andy was small in stature, light in weight and blond of hair with an infectious laugh and sense of humour. He had lived and breathed golf from an early age (His father ran a golf shop in Huntingdon) and, I found out had been taught science by my brother. (This kind of 'I taught your dad' information always ages you and puts you firmly in your place). He also knew some of the people I played football with in my youth and middle age and we exchanged stories about what they were like now and how some of them 'had let themselves go'. I wondered if this statement could also be applied to me. The impressive characteristic of Handy Andy was his boundless enthusiasm that swept you along through good times and bad. First stop: develop your swing off the tee. This sort of worked until he thought I was ready for the next step and promoted me to hitting the ball off the ground, which I knew was the main skill I would have to learn. Result: back to square one and the start of many reverses. But as we hope all women know: it's amazing what a few inches can do once you have adjusted to the size!

What followed was practice, practice, practice. Slowly and surely something started to happen. Handy Andy slowed you down, sped you up, got you to listen to the sound the club made as it whooshed into life on the down swing, concentrated on the hips, the hands, the grip, the angles, the dangles, the take away, the swing plain, the shape, the follow through, the chin, the head, the rotation, the ball position and how you put all these elements together and how if one changed the rest would change. What is impressive is how all this 'torture' was inflicted and I began to wonder if learning golf was a method used in the Spanish Inquisition. Anyway, Handy Andy persisted with the endless patience of a saint. In fact I haven't seen Handy for a while and he may well have joined a monastery to get away from people like me for a quieter life.

'Give me a demo' I said as the realization set in that this game was tricky.

He chose a beaten up old seven iron from the stockpile of used clubs, set up quickly and visibly relaxed. How was he able to hit the ball with such smooth un-missable precision 150 yards to the marker WITH HIS EYES CLOSED? Not once but five times!

'Bloody show off' I thought, but underneath I was really impressed.

Then the breakthrough came (well sort of) on a lovely summer's day two years ago. Like Jesus conducting a miracle (and 'G' golfers often needed a miracle of the same proportions as the raising of Lazarus from the dead), he decided that the only way to get me going was 'the laying on of hands'. Like a masseur in a Turkish bath he pushed, pulled and contorted my creaking body into different positions so I could be more 'dynamic'. Of courses, the reason Handy Andy gave for attacking me up in this very direct fashion was that it was going to improve my golf but at the time you couldn't help wonder whether it was payback for all his pent up frustration that I was unable to do what he was asking.

Handy Andy ready to use
His number one coaching method

'Come here. I'm going to make
your swing more dynamic'

'You alright' he said as something else creaked
I was 'alright'. The basics of a 'swing' had arrived and the only problem was to convert what you were doing in the driving range to the rigors of the golf *curse.* (I thought I'd leave this typo mistake 'curse' uncorrected as it made more sense) AND to add to the woes of real golf, how the bloody hell do you get out of bunkers? … The lessons didn't stretch to that.

As part of the lessons, I did have a go in a special iron contraption that was supposed to educate your swing , 100 percent guaranteed. It was set up next to the pro shop so everyone could see you struggle with the weight of 'the roller' on a system of rails that made you take a 'proper' swing plain. I am not sure whether the contraption helped, but one thing I knew for certain … don't use it just before you pay a game. The heavy roller thing and real clubs are incompatible and any muscle memory you do possess is turned to mush. Going from contraption to real shots on the course was a bit like being drunk. You wanted your body to work in unison but the connections that tied the different parts together were gone, out to lunch or not available.

But thanks to the efforts of 'Handy Andy' I was beginning to understand, perform, compete and enjoy. Like an aging car, I might even go back for a service and some more manipulation to iron out some of the accumulated bad habits.

So where do you go for inspiration?

I can tell you where I have been by giving a plug now for two websites and DVD's I have found very useful. In fact I'd say they have improved my enjoyment and performance to such an extent I have no hesitation in recommending them.

CJ Goeks, who produces a series of great value instructional DVD's that as well as dealing with all aspects of the game give you access to a fantastic series of coaching videos, emails and mini clinics over the internet. For me his analysis and professionalism was a revelation and came at just the right time when I had to make the next moves. Contact details: www.PerfectConnectionGolfSwing.com

Bobby Wilson (himself a golfer of shall we say advancing years, who remains a hall of fame golf drive champion and a member of the 350 yard plus club). He, too, produces some valuable material on DVD and through his web site: www.perfomaxgolf.com Through their tips and instruction I have improved from being desperate to get below 100 to regularly being in the low nineties, to flashing into the mid eighties, to maybe targeting that elusive 80 and enjoying myself in the process ... no matter what.

While on the subject of the internet and new technology, our gang of 'G' golfers are well up with the times. We are thinking of setting up our own website which may well be found at www.geraitricgolfers.com . This site will be set up as a forum for 'G' golfers to tell their stories of triumph and woe and gain tips on growing old while still managing to play. As a specialist site for people of more mature years, it plans to have sponsored links to other useful sites such as

www.playslikeapillock.com

www.medicareforgolfers.co.uk

www.conjunctivitus.com ……. (Now there's a site for sore eyes!)

I am sure that readers of this diary would be brilliant at inventing their own geriatric and golf related websites. Maybe you could enter some below:

Keeping up with the times (part two)

The Karate Kid, being the youngest of our tribe is well up with all new gadgetry and recently purchased a special GPS watch that could not only perform all the functions of a watch but also tell him where he was in the world at any given moment. This is particularly useful for the geriatric golfer as they are prone to forgetting where they are at various times of the day and even what planet they are on. It is often believed for example that the Monarch, when in one of his 'thrashing about' moods, is actually on planet Zog. A quick look at the GPS watch proves that this is the case. When pointed at him it goes into a strange kind of data crash and keeps repeating 'recalculating … recalculating'. Only when he is out of range can the watch be re-set.

This incredible watch which will soon be linked up to Google Earth, also tells you as you approach your ball, the distance to the hole for every golf course in Europe. (with downloadable data from the States available). So when the Kid stands next to you and consults the dial, he will be able to tell you its 120 yards to the flag on the seventeenth and to get to the green you will have to fly the bunker 70 yards away, the ditch containing a protected species of great crested newts slightly further on and the half eaten pigeon that has been dropped by a fox just before the green. And…… just in case you had forgotten, that you are at the Lakeside Lodge golf course in Pidley.

Does this information help our golf? Probably not, in respect of the fact that 'G' golfers have variable swings, with variable distances and variable accuracy. Basically the GPS watch is accurate to within one foot and we are not.

………………………………………………………

So lessons can help but the one lesson that stands out is: keep learning, keep analyzing, change with the times, Enjoy the game and especially the company of your fellow G golfers.

MISCELLANEOUS MAGIC

Big Brother had made it to the eighteenth without too many mishaps and was last up to attempt a drive. Everyone else had done pretty well so the pressure was on for him to perform. Little did we know when he took his place on the tee and looked majestically out at the massive open expanses of the fairway, that he would also take his place in the annals of our geriatric golfing history. In fact a whole chapter could be devoted to this one incident.

The eighteenth is a relatively straightforward par four (stroke index 10). The only problem you can face when driving, is the small lake in front of the tee. This means that any drive has to clear approximately thirty yards to avoid a watery grave before it reaches the open fairway. Not too difficult then.

Now as any 'G' golfer will know, the existence of a hazard has a strange effect on the quality of the shots you make to avoid it. The hazard almost works like a psychological magnet that pulls your shot into its clutches: Ditches, dykes, woods, bunkers and lakes all have the same effect of bewitching your shot and so it was with this stretch of water.

Big Brothers first drive plopped in to the lake, scaring some moorhens who took off into the distance. 'Oooooh Nooooo' he whined in a Scottish accent reminiscent of a howling wolf. 'Three off the tee'

The second shot also suffered from masses of top spin. It skidded through the reeds at the front of the lake and plopped. It was as if a knife had gone through Big Brothers' heart. 'Five off the tee' he said making the long, lonely journey back to his golf bag for another ball. The third shot nearly made it, but plunged into the bank at the other side of the lake and rolled back into the H2O.

'Seven off the tee'.

Now, a situation like this obviously calls for composure, which anybody who knows Big Brother will realize can be in short supply when the chips are down, things are going pear shaped and the walls are tumbling (and other similar clichés of troubles without using the rude one about the shit hitting the fan). Instead of slowing himself down in a peaceful stillness to ponder the mysteries of the perfect swing, Big Brother has an inbuilt tendency to work faster and faster, like a whirling dervish on heat.

This habit of speeding up does your swing, accuracy and tempo no good at all, so in a fog of red mist he went at it again with his fourth attempt. This time the ball did a Barnes Wallis (please see an earlier chapter for definition) and skidded across the lake as if on skis. But once again, it didn't make it to the other side and sunk without trace.

'Nine off the tee'.

As if trapped in the famous Tennyson poem, 'The Charge of the Light Brigade', he could not escape the heat of battle and just kept on going full tilt into the jaws of defeat: If you will forgive the reference to this poem, the story of Bib Brothers' charge into hell went something like this: 'Half a league, half a league, half a league more, Into the valley of death rode Big Brother: Mockery to the left of him, insults to the right. Into the valley of pain he rode again.

Once more he set up just as he had done before and visualized his shot soaring up the fairway. The practice swing looked divine, but the outcome of the fifth shot remained horrific, sucked into the water by siren voices, like the fateful journey of Ulysses trying to find his way home.

'Eleven off the tee'.

I have just realized that there have been a few literary references in the epic account of Big Brothers' excursion into multiple shots, (To Tennyson's poem and Homer's Odyssey so far) so the injection of culture will continue with a nod to Shakespeare and the play Henry the Fifth.

Was Big brother downhearted? …. Well, yes.

Did he try again? … Well yes.

Thinking back, he could have been at the battle of Agincourt summoning up the resources to try again: So there he stood, proudly holding another new ball. He showed it to everyone as if it was the crown jewels and placed it carefully on the tee. You could almost hear him delivering the famous battle speech of Henry V: 'Into the breach once more dear friends: Into the breach. For God, King Hammy and Saint George'.

It may well be an insult to Big Brother to put these English words in his mouth because he is a Scotsman. Maybe the Braveheart

Speech of William Wallace would serve a better purpose. The trouble is, to be effective you have got to imagine it in a Scottish accent

'We may be playing like wee girlies. We may well be crap at rugby, too. It may take us Scotsmen thirteen off the tee, but they canna take away our freedom'

He was indeed thirteen of the tee, but the Gods were at last with him. His sixth drive sailed over the lake, down the fairway and into a parallel ditch. It was the first time that a shot that ended up in a ditch has received a spontaneous round of applause.

Most Geriatric golfers are smart enough to realize that this calamity could happen to us all. Maybe not so badly and it is probable that there is someone out there who can beat our geriatric golf record of thirteen off the tee. If there is, let us know and I am sure Big Brother will not feel so bad.

Needless to say the talk in the bar was what the all time record was was the number of hots off the tee and whether we tried to enter Big Brother in the Guiness book of records, but he looked so depressed that once we dispensed with the ritual humiliation such an epic story brings, we brought him a pint to drown his sorrows, (a bit like he had drowned the balls).

Beyond Relief

When I first heard the expression 'taking relief' I thought it was a code word for a quick pee behind the bushes. I now know it is a welcome way of getting out of trouble within the rules and a topic that is subject to much discussion and variation.

'No relief allowed' claimed the Rugby Man when the Godfather's ball had nestled in a rabbit hole at the top of a bunker.

'But what am I supposed to do?' the godfather asked perplexed.

'Drop a shot'. Said the Rugby man with such authority that it had to be true. Dropping a shot was the only way out. So the godfather with a heavy heart picked his ball out of the hole and with all of us watching, dropped it a clubs length away in the bunker. This painful experience was added to as the Godfather had a double 'adolf' (four shots and still in the bunker) and finally got out on five.

On reflection, this did seem a harsh adjudication as the hazard was animal made but the Godfather took it like a man.

'Definitely relief allowed' said the Monarch whose ball had nestled behind a large tree in a rut of roots with no easy way to hit it in any direction. When this was discussed, the Monarch claimed that the tree was 'staked' because it had just been planted and, therefore, relief was allowable. The fact that the tree was probably over twenty years old and the original stake had become part of the trunk was immaterial. 'If you can see the stake, you can claim the relief.' he dictated. Without further ado the Monarch moved his ball, found a nice resting place away from the tree and took his shot.

'If this was a match, you'd be buggered' stated the Ancient One

'But this isn't a match and you're buggered' said the Monarch as he watched his ball pitch on the green and nestle by the flag for a birdie chance. (Why is it that after a dodgy decision the next shot is mostly perfect, as if the player who has been let off is rubbing it in?)

And so it is that the mysteries of what is and what is not allowable under the rules continues to unfold, depending on who you play with. So what follows could be wrong

A ball high up off the ground in the branches of a tree: Relief not allowed.

The ball balanced precariously on a tri pod of dog turds: Allowed

A ball marooned in free standing water: Maybe not allowed depending where it is

The ball in ground under repair: Allowed (even if the sign has fallen over or been removed)

The ball in a quagmire of mud in which you sink up to your ankles: Not allowed.

A ball hidden by a half eaten pine cone (thrown away by a squirrel). Allowed.

A ball hidden by a half eaten pine cone (thrown away by a rat). Not allowed

A ball moved by the wind before you set up: No penalty

A ball moved by the wind after you set up: Penalty

A shot delayed by the Monarch passing wind: Allowable slow play due to the sympathy vote. You may also be allowed to move away from the area in which the wind was passed if there is not much natural wind!

Definitely Taking Relief: (Weak bladder syndrome)

As you get older, one of nature's cruel tricks is to weaken the bladder so you have to plan all your journeys, activities and water intake by how close you are to a toilet. On the golf course, this can be difficult and there are only a few times that you can coordinate your need to go with arrival back at the club house on the ninth and the eighteen when relief is just a stones throw away and you join the race to the men's room.

In golf' there is also the added pressure of the human body's automatic physical reaction to being nervous (a condition that can be brought about by the challenges of the game), when primitive survival instincts kick in and you a compelled by fear to (pardon the expression) excrete in readiness for fight or flight.

You are then faced with the curious situation of having just gone to the toilet before the start of the round, only to find yourself two minutes later nervously standing on the first tee and wanting to 'go again.'

Trying to 'relax' is a prerequisite of a decent shot, so you force the pressure back only to have it increase again before your second shot like an impending flood about to overflow a dam. The pain can be palpable. Once again you wiggle your knees and bob up and down a bit and somehow these curious movements delay the urge to go. That is until you can keep it in no longer, rush to the nearest wooded area and struggle to gain access to your waterworks using the following formula:

The more you want to go, the harder it gets to find your equipment, whip it out and get on with it. Access also becomes especially difficult in winter when the part of your body involved in this process shrinks and multiple layers of clothing delays your search. This panic to pee can also be accompanied by cries of agony as you try hard not to wet yourself before the one eyed snake is given some air.

For medical reasons, often linked to the drugs we are on, some 'G' golfers suffer more than others from weak and leaky bladder syndrome and, being the friends we are, we make allowances. Even the tell tale signs of a trail of damp down the trouser leg after a particularly hard shot or inability to find a secluded area to relieve yourself are disregarded and forgiven.

Trail of damp down the trouser leg can also occur because at our age, you sometimes think you have finished when you haven't. This, apart from being wet and uncomfortable in the upper and lower leg region is also highly embarrassing and means that you try not to walk with the others until you have dried off. If this is not possible, you may have to walk like the Hunchback of Notre Dame, dragging one leg behind the other to make sure the trail of damp is hidden.

It is also interesting to note that weak bladder syndrome (even if you haven't got it) is catching. Once one person succumbs to the call of nature, the others follow as if it's compulsory for you to mark out your territory. Like lined up dominoes, once one is tipped into action the others follow, spurred on by the look of relief on his face. This is especially true on the thirteenth where there must be a long history of people relieving themselves behind the wooden shelter that stands to the side of the tee. It's secluded. It stinks, and the grass around the area looks like it's been poisoned. No wild life dares venture there. There is no doubt that we men are responsible for many atrocities on the golf course.

Winter warmers

Come rain, come shine, come freeze come thaw, the geriatric golfer will be out on the course playing their game. There is no 'off season' and no possible weather condition that will get in the way of their wish to play and very few occasions when the weather will win.

It was on a particularly bad day one winter, when the temperature was well into the minuses and there was a light covering of snow on the ground that a group of delegates on a conference at the club house looked out from the breakfast area and saw a trail of 'G' golfers making their way in single file to the first tee.

Picture the scene. There were the delegates in the warm, in normal dress tucking into a full English breakfast. There we were outside in the cold, with so many multiple layers that we looked like Michelin Men (as wide as we were tall with strange bulges all over our bodies) and were hardly able to move. Like Scott of the Antarctic we put on that typical British stiff upper lip (This couldn't be helped because the upper lip was frozen solid) and unable to talk or walk properly, we made it to the first tee.

One of the delegates watching us from the warmth of the club house mouthed that immortal British phrase 'What the f*** are they doing?' and about twenty heads around him turned in silence to watch this band of stupid buggers take on the elements.

Apart from being unable to communicate except in sign language, the first problem was trying to put the tee into the ground. We had forgotten the hammer drill and looked round for alternatives. Maybe we could make a little pile of snow. Maybe we would put the driver away and go to work with a lesser club. It was then Big Brother came to the rescue and from his pocket produced a cone like piece of plastic that could be constructed to form a platform at different levels. The 'cone' was brilliant and whenever there is a danger of frost, there he is ready with his contraption.

Of course, preparing for a game in the depths of winter also puts extra pressure on 'G' golfers because it often puts them in the embarrassing position of having to be seen by their wives in strange figure hugging long johns. Even super fit hunks look fairly peculiar in these undergarments so the sight of old men with bulbous tummies with match stick legs underneath and knobbly knees in the middle must really be a turn off.

Winter Bounce

It is always interesting to play on frozen ground as even flat fairways and flush greens have a life of their own that defies logic.

'Did you see that?' said the Professor as what would have been a brilliant shot under 'normal' conditions hits the front of the green and immediately launches into orbit, taking the ball through the green and out of bounds in one bounce.

'What happened to that?' asks Big Brother as a shot down the fairway hits some sort of frozen divot and takes off at ninety degrees to its starting direction.

And the iced up greens are a lottery as the frost collects on your ball and turns it into an immovable object or a thawed out patch speeds it up.

'It all adds to the joy of life' says the Karate Kid. And for geriatric golfers, in a strange way, it does.

Winter Greens

What on earth can be interesting about winter greens? Well, only the fact that sometimes you don't know they are there. As a novice, 'winter greens' were an unexplained phenomenon. For all I knew this expression could have been about Brusell sprouts or a particular variety of cabbage.

'We're on winter greens' said Big Brother on the first

I did not know what he meant. So we all took our normal shot down the fairway of a par five. Having driven badly (a characteristic of my early days of playing this game), I was first in line to take the second shot and set up with a five wood. More by luck than judgment I creamed a beauty straight down the fairway. This was probably my best shot I had ever made up to this point in my career, and I stepped back to admire it.

'Great shot' said Big Brother 'but the winter green is over there'

He pointed to a tiny circle of grass off the main fairway where my ball was lying and **on the other side of a lake** right opposite the normal green. Needless to say, all their second shots were sent in the right direction towards this hidden 'winter green' and to the correct side of the lake.

'You might have told me' I said wondering, with my lack of skill, how I was going to get my third shot across the lake and onto the adjacent grass.

'That wouldn't have been so much fun' was the reply

There was no pity shown as every shot I took went into the water. 'Pick it up' said Big Brother. 'That will teach you'. Golf can be a cruel sport and even crueler when you fellow golfers set you up and watch you suffer.

I remain psychologically scarred.

The Day of the Divot / What a SOD.

Most golfers sometime in their career will have taken a divot. For professional golfers this is a necessary part of the game, when the divot is taken <u>after</u> the ball. It is apparently the hallmark of a clean strike and a good shot that seems beyond the reach of mere amateurs. For some reason 'G' golfers are unable to develop this skill and inevitably end up taking a huge divot or tell tale skid marks before the ball. The outcomes are usually not very good. As well as stunning the left arm into submission, the following can happen:

The divot flies further than the ball and you wish the hole was big enough to swallow you up.

The contact with the ground pulls the club face around and ends up sending the ball way off target making you look even worse than you actually are.

But can you beat this: (Maybe you can?) It was on the thirteenth. Godfather set up for his second shot in the middle of the fairway with a seven iron. The practice swing was smoother than we are normally used to and the moment came for him to find the green. The swing was low and slow. There was a dull thud. Somehow the club face had cut into the turf before the ball, dislodged a piece about fifteen centimeters square and without the sod leaving the ground folded it over the top of the ball <u>without moving it.</u> It was pretty close to a miracle, but then again the Godfather is always praying for one of those.

The Godfather looked down the fairway wondering where his ball had gone, completely oblivious to the fact it was still in the same place and hidden under the clump of earth his club had scythed and hinged. As it was a cold day, we took pity on him and allowed it as a practice shot. He uncovered his ball being careful not to move it, (blind eyes were turned), replaced the divot, took another shot and ended up in the bunker.

Summer Magic

With my limited experience it seems that summer brings better scores as the elements favour distance, run and smoother greens. But there is a downside to summer we all have to be aware of:

The sight of geriatric golfers' legs.

I don't know what it is about getting older, but those once unblemished bits of flesh and bone that carry you around suddenly begin to look like grafted on additions from a Frankenstein experiment. The skin goes blotchy, the elasticity that once held the skin tight round well defined muscles gives up its efforts and morphs into wrinkly grooves and the aging veins that criss cross mainly white legs begin to resemble a road map. Some of us with medical conditions and taking rat poison also bruise more easily, so after the slightest touches, our skin begins to resemble purple blotched wall paper. There is no peace in growing old, just a series of psychological adjustments

But we can cope with any downside because the summer allows us to become men of fashion. Gone are the dowdy colours of winter and out come the multi coloured shirts, shorts, jumpers and socks that adorn the golf course in summer. In the summer the Dandy's come out to play, and if we can't play golf very well, at least we can look the part.

In fact you could say, (as the Kinks sang about in their sixties hit), we become dedicated followers of fashion. (With apologies to Ray Davies and to the tune that all existing British geriatric golfers of a certain age will remember)

We see him here
We see him there
On the first green
Without a care
He looks the part,
It's quite an art
No bogies to declare
When he's a dedicated follower of fashion

And when he struts
On to the tee
He looks so good
It's a mystery
So if you want to play
This game of golf
Make sure that all can see
That you're a dedicated follower of fashion

CHORUS

Oh yes you are
Oh yes you are
When you look so fine

We all want you to play well
But when the Gods of golf
Take a look at you
They'll bugger up your shot
You're just a dedicated follower of fashion

BACK TO THE TUNE!

From designer top
To coloured cap
You look so good
But your shots are crap
If only you could
Strike the ball
To match the way you look
You'd be a dedicated follower of fashion

And so you soak
Up summer sun
It's how you 'feel'
You're number one
The time has come
To flash more cash
Buy clothes to have your fun
'Cos you're a dedicated follower of fashion

The ladies, too, take up the summer air of freedom and begin to wear skimpier tops and more revealing bottoms. (And why is it that female legs don't look as worn away by time as male legs? … Maybe we ought to start using regenerating creams, potions and fillers). This female 'flashing' can, of course, provide a distraction as you wend your way around the course and you may be more likely to let a group of women play through because of this 'visual' factor. There is also no doubt that when you sit outside the club house at the end of your round and watch a female foursome come onto the eighteenth green that the silence increases and your attention wanders as the ladies bend down to line up their shots.

This discussion is not going in the right direction so let's introduce another distraction:

Killer wasps

You are back at the clubhouse. It is inevitable that just as you sit down to enjoy a cold beer (or orange juice if you are driving) that as soon as you are comfortable, one wasp will spy your drink, do a waggle dance and call her mates. (I think I am right in saying that all worker bees and wasps are female). And so the hunting instinct takes over as you make sure the pathway to your mouth is bee free between sips. You set traps with inverted glasses, you swish them away onto the person sitting next to you, who swishes them back with a much better swing than he ever displayed on the golf course. You use your score card as a wasp crusher or a wasp basher and put it to much better use than keeping your score. You finally lose concentration and energy and give up, letting the wasp share in the nectar that you thought was just for you.

What else does summer bring to occupy the 'G' golfer? ...... Thicker rough. More water intake, sweating and suntan lotion in the eyes. The inability to see where your ball went if you are playing into the sun, car temperatures that cook you when you get in after a game, melting chocolate in your 'goody' bag. Hay fever. Leaves on trees! (Apparently a tree if full leaf is 90 percent air, so why is it that any shot into 90 percent air seems to be deflected by the 10 percent of substance?). Birds trying to have sex everywhere while you are trying to take your shot. Thunder and lightning, although in my two years of playing this has never happened.

As you may have gathered, this diary has just morphed into an essential characteristic of a geriatric golfer ..... We are frequently moaning old buggers who are so full of themselves they even try to change the world as they meander around he golf course, discuss problems of national and international importance and offer wonderful solutions.

'Bloody government. Shoot the lot of them.'

'Have you seen what they want to do with pensions?'

'You know what they ought to do to shorten the dole queues don't you? ..... Get people to stand closer together!'

And as Big Brother and The Monarch are ex- RAF personnel, they often use their wisdom to discuss the armed services. Here's one example:

'How do you know they are going to close down the local RAF base?

'The Ministry of Defence has just announced a major refurbishment project'

It's probably just as well we are not in decision making positions any more! And it maybe the invocation of along lost memory: That we were useful once.

Such are the joys of summer. Maybe you have some more?

A Little Bit of Club Throwing

No diary about this game of golf would be complete without a brief mention of the skills of club throwing, twirling, bashing and thrashing. We have all seen it, all experienced it and maybe some of us have even done it.

Our gang of geriatric golfers has its own expert and you may have guessed it is the Monarch of the Glen. What follows is a brief description of his techniques which show him to be at the pinnacle of his career as our number one club thrower. We would back him against all comers.

1. *The under arm lob*: This is often reserved for the putter when one of his putts goes astray. Only once has this club ever actually landed on the green and taken a divot out of the sacred turf, which shows his ability to control distance, speed and accuracy. In fact if the Monarch could control his actual putts with the same skill as he controls his putter lob, he would probably be unbeatable.

2. *The forward shunt*: This frequently follows a bad drive where the driver is propelled forward to the right hand side of the tee. This is carefully placed so as to offer no threat to other players and is often accompanied by a torrent of expletives.

3. *The downward slap:* Only reserved for iron shots where the club is bounced into submission that it was the clubs fault that the shot did not go where it was supposed to and not the player. This method has its origins from the comedy series Fawlty Towers, where Basil is seen threatening the a clapped out car and thrashing it when it doesn't start.

4. *The rotational lunge:* For use with woods and rescue clubs where the club is swung several times around the body in a circular motion before being launched like a discus. This can be one of the

most dangerous of his club throwing repertoire so signs that it is about to happen are closely observed by fellow golfers. These signs can include a change of facial colour from white to crimson; the head to toe shaking of the body as if he is experiencing an electric shock; or the bowing of his head as if in prayer

5. *The I'm aiming for my trolley flick:* This is less violent than other methods where from a variable distance, the Monarch tries to get his club in his bag with one throw. This is seldom successful in that the club often clatters his expensive motorized trolley. Several of the 'G' golfers have suggested this is probably the main reason that it keeps breaking down.

6. *The I'm going home kick:* Although there are other variations of the Monarch's considerable club throwing skill, we will end with this one. A bit like the Monarch, as when he drops the club and kicks it towards his trolley, this is a sure sign that he will not finish the round, leave early and go home. This is often accompanied by a recurrence of old rugby injuries.

I also need to admit, here, that not long after I started playing, (a few weeks) the Monarch helped me out by offering me his old Taylor Made driver for ten pounds. He had bought another 'Big Bertha' and was anxious to move his old one on. This seemed like a bargain and was a bargain. On close observation of this club you could see the battle scars of it being bashed, hurled and lobbed with a curious circular imprint shaped like a bottle top on the edge of the titanium head. To be able to put an imprint in Titanium, the hardest metal know to man, is unique and a testament to the Monarchs club bashing skills. But this club has done me proud. So thanks, Monarch. I promise to treat the club with care and hand it on as a family heir loom long after I am gone.

In fact that thought of 'going' to that great golf club in the sky opens a new area of consideration for the 'G' Golfer. What happens to their clubs, trolleys, clothes and score cards when they go to that big golf club in the sky?

Although it's a morbid thought, the time has come to deal with it

God: '*What makes you think you deserve to come in here, then?'*

Golfer: *'My handicap is 28!'*

The shots that make it all worth it

Before the final chapter, let's think about the times when the shots you planned came off and you clench your fist in triumph rather than that normal feeling of clenching the buttocks in fear. Go on, do yourself a favour. Re-live those shots now as you trawl the memory banks. You know it will do you good: The long putt that wove in an 'S' shape through a tricky green before plopping in the hole to a fist pumping celebration and the wonder of your mates; The smooth drive that for some reason took off at the perfect launch angle, flew down the fairway and ended up forty yards further than normal; (How you managed to achieve this triumph you will never know, but it happened). The approach shot that any professional would have been proud of as it lands at the lip of the green and rolls inexorably towards the hole. The perfect chip, the supreme lay up, the exquisite bunker shot, the miraculous get of trouble shot, the first time you managed to draw a shot ON PURPOSE; the first time you got back spin on the ball.

We all have such magic moments in our locker and they sustain us with wonderful memories that something we tried to do on a golf course, actually worked. These magic moments coupled with the natural resilience of a golfer keep us coming back for more and they serve as a constant reminder that, maybe, we can do it again.

We might even revel in the thought that on our home track that we have played on for years, we may have actually made par on every hole on the course and a birdie on many. Put all these magic moments together and on a good day you could even be a scratch golfer. (The great Sam Torrence comment 'Dream on' comes to mind... and by the way this is the title of another great book on golf by John Richardson, where a very ordinary golfer who shoots 100 plus is challenged to save 33 strokes and break par within a year. What a lovely dream! You'll have to read it to find out if it comes true.)

Is there a moral to this story? Never forget that no matter how erratic we are, we have all tasted success. And more importantly, even if the golf has been patchy, frustrating, unfathomable and all the other words for 'difficult' you can think of, you will also have made some brilliant friendships that makes up for the pain.

A Final poem (with thanks to Ben)

In my hand I hold a ball,
White and dimpled, rather small.
Oh how bland it does appear,
This harmless looking little sphere.
By its size, I could not guess
The awesome strength it does possess.
But since I fell beneath its spell
I've wandered through the gates of hell.
My life has not been quite the same
Since I choose to play this stupid game.
It rules my mind for hours on end,
A fortune it has made me spend.
It has made me curse, it has made me cry,
And hate myself and want to die.
It promised me a thing called 'par'
If I hit it straight and far.
To master such a tiny ball
Should not be very hard at all.
But my desires the ball refuses
And does exactly as **it** chooses.
It hooks, and slices, dribbles, dies,

And disappears before my eyes.
Often it will have a whim
To hit a tree or take a swim.
With miles of grass on which to land,
It finds a tiny patch of sand.
Then has me offering up my soul
If only it would find the hole.
It's made me whimper like a pup
And swear that I will give it up,
And take to drink to ease my sorrow
But this ball knows… I'll be back tomorrow.

So stand proud you noble swingers of clubs and losers of balls. A recent study found the average golfer walks about 900 miles a year. Another study found golfers drink, on average, 22 gallons of alcohol a year. That means the average golfer gets about 41 miles to the gallon!

Such efficiency … makes you feel like a hybrid.

POSTSCRIPT

Since the publication of this diary the 'escapades' (with the main emphasis on the word 'escape') have continued, and back in May 2012, the event we have all dreamed of after a heavy night on the alcohol finally occurred. I am, of course referring to that most elusive shot in golf: .... the hole in one. It was on the third (par 3), approximately 160 yards to the green which is heavily protected by a well located bunker (Well located for the likes of our group, who usually end up in it or the woods to the right or left of a very narrow fairway)

The Novice took a six iron, (he always tries to lay up on this hole and jump the bunker on his second shot) but on this occasion, a sweet strike sent the ball sailing high and straight. 'If that lands on the green it will be a good shot' said the novice who saw his ball land on flat stuff and disappear over a slight rise.

'I think that's in the hole' said the professor getting excited (a rarely seen event)

'Nooooo, it's gone through the green' said the novice peering into the distance

'I'm telling you. It's in the hole'

The enthusiasm of the professor and the godfather was hard to contain and they set off with a bounce towards the pin, largely ignoring their balls; (easy to do when they are lost).

'Can't see your ball' they said in unison. 'We're telling you it's in the hole.'

'Noooo'

'Want a bet?'

'How much?'

There was no response to this pecuniary challenge as the chance of losing money is a hard call for those of us who grew up on rationing after the war. The professor made a beeline for the flag. 'There it is he said' peering in and pulling it out. 'Amazing. After all these years I can actually say I've played with someone who's got a hole in one.'

As it was the week of the BMW British Open at Wentworth, I called in to the club house after the round (a ninety) to get the keys to my new seven series top of the range motor, only to learn that the only prize I was likely to get was a large bill in the clubhouse where everyone was waiting for a drink.

But the memory of this special day survives and will accompany our little group through their dotage, through the inevitable stay at the old peoples home and maybe even to the grave. To commemorate this achievement, the ball that made this eventful journey sits in a special place on the mantle piece

'Dust trap' says the novice's wife who doesn't understand the significance of these things and has to clean round it. 'When you're gone, I won't want it. It will end up in your coffin along with the golf shoes you never clean!'

'What a way to go' said the Novice thinking about his final journey … 'with a tiny white dimpled ball that travelled 160 yards and ended up in a three inch hole in the ground and Bing Crosby singing S*traight down the middle*'

'It's a bloody Dunlop' said big brother on seeing it for the first time. 'You could have done it with a decent ball!'

The Novice didn't say anything

Needless to say, the next week all eyes were on my tee shot on the third. It ended up in the bunker, one unsuccessful escape shot and a double bogey. How the mighty are fallen.

Just like the epics of old and as is customary in this journal, this rare event is calling out to be celebrated in verse (or as the readers might refer to it .. bad to verse!)

It was on the third at Lakeside
The Godfather led the way
He sliced his shot into the woods
'That's crap' I heard him say

Next up came the professor
He drove it high and straight
It plugged into the bunker
'Just my luck' he said 'That's fate!'

Then came the shot to end all shots
The dream to end all dreams
The novice hit a beauty

And it landed on the green

'Not only on the green' they said
'It's heading for the pin
You one off jammy bastard
The buggers going in'

And in it went, one sixty yards
For once, you are a star
What a pity there's no TV crew
What a pity there's no car

T'was a shot you will remember
And the story never ends
The day you got a hole in one
The witnesses, your friends.

So what about your hole in one stories?

DRIVING TOWARDS A SUNSET

Although this image presents an optimistic view of playing golf in the latter years of your life, I thought I would end with it, knowing that the sun *will* get lower and lower on the horizon until one day it will set completely on your golf career and then on you.

This may sound depressing, but in my opinion, once you accept that this inevitable journey will take place, you are better equipped to face the facts and make the most of what you've got. As mentioned throughout this diary of events, as geriatric golfers (or 'seniors' to make it sound more acceptable), we *will* be challenged by the ageing process and the physical nature of the game. In fact we can count ourselves lucky that golf can be played with so much enjoyment for so long in our lives.

In this regard I would like to pay a massive compliment the Godfather. Following a major medical issue a decade ago he has kept going against the odds. He has turned up, played badly, played well, amused us all, amused himself, and done all this with good humour and a just a small smattering of swear words. What a role model he is to 'G' golfers everywhere. You will all have your role models that keep you going. The Godfather is ours. He is our version of Tom Watson (without playing so well, of course)

I am so pleased that the Godfather introduced me to this game just over two years ago. It's a focus. It's a laugh. It's a blessing (of sorts). And it has given me the huge privilege of knocking about with a brilliant crew of resilient friends, fellow 'geriatric' golfers, frequent achievers and fellow sufferers.

That's enough torture for one day!

I hope you have enjoyed this account of some of our exploits and that it has made you think of your own adventures and the good times you have had and will have.

Here's to the future

The Novice

Harry Pearce

Printed in Great Britain
by Amazon.co.uk, Ltd.,
Marston Gate.